FATHERHOOD

WHAT IT IS AND WHAT IT'S FOR

FATHERHOOD

WHAT IT IS AND WHAT IT'S FOR

TONY PAYNE

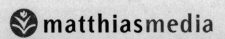

Fatherhood
© Matthias Media 2004

Published in the United Kingdom by:
The Good Book Company
Telephone: 0845-225-0880
Facsimile: 0845-225-0990
Email: admin@thegoodbook.co.uk
Internet: www.thegoodbook.co.uk

ISBN 1 876326 99 9

Cover design and typesetting by Lankshear Design Pty Ltd.

Printed in the UK by Bookmarque

Dedication

To Alison, wife, best friend and super-mum,
and to our little tribe—Gemma, Chloë, Miriam,
Luke and Nicholas—with apologies for having taken
so long to learn some of the lessons of this book.

CONTENTS

1. Mind games 9

Part I: What is fatherhood?

2. The fruit of his body 19
3. A river to his people 31
4. The power to serve 47
5. Practical authority 61
6. The Captain and the Nice-Guy 83

Part II: What's it all for?

7. Why bother? 93
8. The day everything changed 105
9. The disciple 115
10. Taking them with you 141
11. Be a man 171

Further reading 175

CHAPTER 1

MIND GAMES

JUDGING BY THE many books on 'fatherhood' and 'manhood' that I've read over the past three years, there are some standard ways to get a book like this started.

I could kick off with some funny and endearing stories about my own fumbling efforts at being a dad over the past 16 years, perhaps involving mishaps with dirty nappies or family dinners that turned into circuses.

Or I could tell you a story about my own Dad, and what sort of man he was. I could speak of how his strong, quiet presence was the rock on which our family was built, and how his death eleven years ago broke my heart in a way that I never imagined that it would.

Or perhaps I could start with some social analysis: "Living as we do in the wake of feminism, traditional gender roles and distinctions have been overturned in our society. 'Fatherhood' is in crisis. And the dimensions of that crisis grow daily more alarming …". I could follow this with statistics on how lack of good fathering is breeding a generation of insecure, overweight good-for-nothings who do little more than complain, text one another and improve their PlayStation high scores.

These and many other possible intros could keep us going quite happily for several pages.

But the truth is: I don't think you need a lot of convincing to read a book about fatherhood. Nor do I think you need a long introduction about the challenges of being a dad. You and I both know that it's tough. It's demanding and tiring and infuriating, as well as being just about the best thing most of us have ever done. And do we feel like we do a good job—no, make that an *adequate* job? I haven't met many dads who feel confident to say they do.

It may be small comfort, but I think it's always been this way. Adam, after all, had some fairly major squabbles to sort out between his boys. (You can just hear Eve saying, "Look, I *told* you to have a talk to Cain about his anger management. Didn't I tell you? But you were too busy working back late on the thistles and thorns to take any notice.") I don't think we're the first generation in the history of the world to feel that being a father is no easy task.

However, it's also true to say that being a dad at the opening of the 21st century does pose some special challenges. Without reverting to the social analysis intro, our community desperately needs to create or rediscover a version of 'fatherhood' that works in the modern world. It's widely recognized that there *is* something of a fatherhood crisis in our culture, and that two factors in particular are responsible.

One is the simple fact that, in our culture, the vast majority of fathers find themselves separated from their children for most of their waking lives. For those who suffer the heartbreak of marriage breakdown, the separation is obvious and usually drastic. But even those of us who manage to stay married don't see much of our kids. We go to work; they go to school. If we're lucky, our paths might cross for a brief hectic hour at night. And on the weekends, in between everything that has to be done to keep the household moving, there is precious little time for being with our kids. Even if we knew what it was that we should do as fathers, we're not sure when we're going to find the time to do it. It wasn't always like this, and the fact that it *is* now like this creates some particular challenges.

The second is that after the feminist revolution of the past 30 years, no-one's exactly sure these days what a 'father' is, and what he should do. To suggest that he's the head of the household, the breadwinner who brings home the bacon, is to invite a stiletto to the instep. But what is he then? Is he any different from a 'mother', apart from some variations in plumbing? Do modern families have two mums or two dads? Or have we evolved a new species: the 'mad' (or should that be the 'dum')?

Judging by the flood of books on 'manhood' and 'fatherhood' that keep washing over us, I'm not the only one noticing these things, or trying to say something about them. But what I want to do in this book is a little different from most others on the subject.

I want to change your mind.

Like most sports, and indeed most activities in life, the mental game is where 85% of fathering takes place. Becoming a good father is not about learning five practical handy techniques that can be pulled out of the kitbag whenever they're needed. It's a mind game. It's about having a set of attitudes and ideas that shape what you do in the thousands of different situations you find yourself in as a dad. Every child is different. Every day is different. And each day, there's a new challenge, a new situation in which to think: Now what am I supposed to do about this?

Our actions are shaped and driven by our mind, by the core beliefs, assumptions and rules of thumb that we've acquired over the years. We get these from our parents and upbringing, from our education, from our religious or political beliefs, from the papers we read or the TV programs we watch, from our mates, or just from trial and error.

We all have a mental grid like this. We filter our perceptions of the world and daily life through it. It shapes and drives the way we act. Even those of you who may at this point be thinking, "What a load of rubbish—I don't have a mental grid or mindset; I just follow common sense" are demonstrating the particular mental grid or set of beliefs that you have (in this case, one that distrusts thinking about things too much, and assumes that nearly all situations have simple 'common sense' or 'practical' solutions).

In the course of this book, I want to change your mind about fathering. I want to change the way you think about it, both consciously and instinctively. And if I succeed, it will change the way you act every day in a thousand ways. It will make you a better father.

I want to change your mind about two particular things.

First of all, I want to change your thinking about what fatherhood *is*. I want to persuade you first of all that there is such a thing as 'fatherhood', and that it has a certain shape, a certain look to it (that doesn't have any necessary connection to cardigans, people-carriers or golf, excellent though each of those things are). I'll be arguing that because the God who made the universe also constructed the thing we call 'fatherhood', it has certain stubborn characteristics. There *is* a unique role for fathers to play in our families and in our community, and that role takes its characteristics from how God designed fatherhood to be.

(You're not seeing things. The word 'God' did appear twice in that last paragraph. If this is a surprise to you, please read the 'Special Note to Atheist, Agnostic or

Otherwise-Spiritually-Committed Readers' at the end of this introduction.)

The second and slightly more radical thing I want to do is show that fatherhood not only has certain characteristics, but has a particular *purpose*. I want to change your mind about what fatherhood is *for*. This may not be something that you've thought a whole lot about. Just getting through the week with a minimum of grief is usually enough to satisfy most of us. But God not only made fatherhood to be a certain way, he made it with a goal in mind. In other words, your job as a father is not simply to *be* a father, but to achieve certain things as a father. You have an assignment, a mission. The second half of this book is all about that mission.

Of course the question you should be asking by now is: 'What makes your mental grid any better than mine? What gives you the right to assume that your way of thinking is so superior that you should try to impose it upon me?'

My answer would be: if it is God's grid that I manage to insert into your brain, then that would be worth having. If it is merely my own musings and opinions, you might as well save the time and get back to the TV—after all, there is professional sport being played somewhere on the planet at this very moment, and you are missing it. I may fail, of course, to rightly or clearly explain God's view of fatherhood from the Bible (which is where he reveals it). You can check that by reading the Bible for yourself. But if I do manage to explain things clearly, then God's word has the power to transform your mind and to make it correspond more closely to reality. As the Creator of the world, God is in a remarkably good position to tell us how to live in it, in this area of fatherhood and in all others. His truth can change your mind, and turn you into something approaching a real father.

• • •

Special Note to Atheist, Agnostic or Otherwise-Spiritually-Committed Readers

The book that you're holding, like all books, springs from a particular view of the world. In this case, it's a Christian view of the world.

There's every chance that you don't fully understand what a 'Christian' world view is—for example, most people I've talked to think it's got something to do with being moralistic and going to church and hoping that God will be sufficiently impressed by your good deeds to let you into heaven. This is not even close. I hope that as you read on, you might gain some appreciation of what the Christian Scriptures actually teach.

In fact, the quotations from the Bible that are sprinkled

throughout this book may take some getting used to, if you haven't read many books by Christian authors before. The quotations are there for the reason noted above; namely, that what I am trying to do is uncover and explain what *God* thinks about fatherhood, and the Christian view is that the Bible is where those thoughts are found.

Whether you already know quite a bit about Christianity or not, and whether you're mildly-pro, vigorously-anti or mostly-couldn't-care-less, I hope that you'll do the intelligent thing and read on with an open mind. I think you might be a little surprised by what you find. The various parts of the Bible we'll be looking at teach some extraordinarily helpful things about fatherhood. Whether or not you want to go with the whole package, you're bound to pick up some useful ideas.

PART I
WHAT IS FATHERHOOD?

CHAPTER 2
THE FRUIT OF HIS BODY

I DON'T KNOW IF you've ever tried to maintain a serious conversation with someone while they are attacking your private parts with a knife, but that's what I found myself doing one early summer morning in 1996.

It happened after the birth of our fifth child. My wife and I decided that it was definitely time for 'something to be done', and so I duly trotted off to a local vasectomy clinic to be 'done', as we modern men do. (And no, the doctor was not a microsurgeon.)

As I filled out the extensive questionnaire/application form in the crowded waiting room, I looked around and saw with some surprise that I was the only man present. The rest were young women, all sitting like me with a form on their laps, most of them with mothers or other older supporters beside them. None of them were smiling, but then I can't say I was either. Slowly the awful truth dawned on me that the clinic not only provided services for those not wishing to conceive children, but also for those who already had and wished they hadn't.

Something on my application form must have made the doctor twig that I was a Christian. Perhaps it was 'Occupation: writer of books about Jesus Christ'. In any case, he asked me, quite out of the blue, what I thought of abortion.

"I think it's a stain on our social conscience, a terrible tragedy for many women, and a merciless crushing of the weak by the strong for their own convenience" is what I wished I'd said. Instead, having other matters like the future of my manhood on my mind, I stammered something about being against it.

"Tell me", he said, "as a Christian, would it make any difference to you if the termination of the foetus took place not by active surgical intervention but through the creation of certain conditions whereby the woman's body itself terminated the pregnancy?"

I told him that it sounded like a fudge, and we proceeded to discuss the ethics of abortion, and the nature of the Christian opposition to it. He was a thoughtful man, and was interested that the Protestant or Reformation basis for opposing abortion was different from the Roman Catholic basis, and so the conversation continued—all the way to the operating table where, under a local anaesthetic and with the relevant areas discreetly covered, we continued to talk about the ethics of reproduction, while he hacked away at the family jewels.

"Tin-snips; pliers; blowtorch", he would say to the nurse, and then to me, "So you're saying that ever since Aquinas, Catholics have based their view of sex on natural law…".

• • •

As I LIMPED HOME, I thought about the young women in the waiting room. Where were the boyfriends or husbands? Where were the fathers of those little barely-formed bundles of life? Did they know or care? Had they pressured the women to have the abortions? Or did their absence say it all—they didn't want anything to do with the whole thing, and so the women were faced with raising the child alone or terminating its existence alone?

My visit to the vasectomy/abortion clinic was like a parable of modern reproduction. The contribution of fathers to the making of the babies is small and easily dispensed with. We throw in a couple of drops of fluid and then we're out of there, so to speak. And should we wish to stop making that contribution, a little snip-snip and the job is done.

The real business of reproduction belongs to women. And it is they who must bear the cost and responsibility of bearing the child, or deciding not to. As the abortion debate has so strongly emphasized, many modern women see the foetus as part of their own bodies, as something which belongs to them, and over which they have the power of life and death.

Having children is women's business. The technology of reproduction in our world only reinforces this. It is now very possible to conceive and give birth without the involvement of a father at all, apart from some anonymous sperm donation.

It's as if (in our way of thinking about it) mothers are the principals in the baby-making business, and fathers are junior partners who have a minor role to play in the process.

Of course, this suits a lot of men just fine. They are only too happy to distance themselves from the whole mess, and to thereby diminish any responsibility they might have for the children. And it suits some women quite well too, who find men more trouble then they're worth, and would be just as happy to raise children without them.

However, most men and women seem to regard the gradual sidelining of men in the baby-production business as a net loss. The less fathers feel that their role is central and important, the less likely they are to roll up their sleeves and play an active and helpful part in the raising of the child.

• • •

ALL OF WHICH MAKES the view of fathering we see in the Bible seem very different—because one of the things that strikes you straight away as you read the Bible is that fathers are, if anything, the *senior* partners in the baby-production business. To be a father, in the biblical world view, is to be a life-giver. Fathers are the seed-sowers, the 'begetters' of offspring. In the Bible's way of thinking, the life principle is in the man's 'seed', which is planted in the fertile ground of the woman's womb, and with God's blessing eventually produces fruit.

Now there isn't a chapter in the Bible headed 'Reproduction: Bible's unique view of', that summarizes all this. It's a way of thinking that is revealed in many different parts of the Bible almost incidentally, in the midst of other stories.

For example, when that most depressed of the biblical authors, Job, looks back on the very beginnings of his life (in order to loathe it and wish he'd never been born), he says to God:

> Did you not pour me out like milk and curdle me
> like cheese?
> You clothed me with skin and flesh,
> and knit me together with bones and sinews.
> (Job 10:10–11)

The image is of the milk (i.e. the semen) 'curdling' in the

mothers womb, and becoming something solid, a body knit together with bones and sinews and clothed with skin and flesh. From our 21st century point of view, this doesn't sound quite right. It's not just the 'milk' supplied by the father that creates the omelette. We know about the egg that the woman brings to the process. We've seen those photos of the seemingly huge globular ovum surrounded by thousands of little tadpoles all trying to be the lucky one.

However, strict anatomical details aside, Job's description is a powerful image of the role of the father's seed in the conception of children. And it lies behind the biblical authors' view of children as the offspring not only of the mother (obviously enough) but especially of the father.

We see it in the saga of Abraham. There comes a point in that story where Abraham (or Abram as he is still called at this stage) is feeling none too sure about whether God is going to fulfil his promise to him. You may remember that God had promised to make Abram into a great nation, and that he would have many descendants. The only minor technical difficulty was that Abram and his wife Sarah were childless, and were getting well past the age when they could reasonably expect to have children. And so in Genesis 15, Abram cries out to God and says:

> "O Lord GOD, what will you give me, for I continue child-
> less, and the heir of my house is Eliezer of Damascus? …

Behold, you have given me no offspring, and a member of my household will be my heir." (Gen 15:2-3)

God reassures Abram by telling him:

"This man shall not be your heir; what will *come out of your own belly* will be your heir." (Gen 15:4, my translation)

Apart from that rather dismal movie *Junior*, in which Arnold Schwarzenegger played a man who becomes pregnant, we don't tend to think of children coming out of their father's belly. Yet for the writer of Genesis, it was just as natural to talk of a child coming out of a father's belly as to say that it came out of the mother's belly. Just a few chapters later, when Abraham's daughter-in-law Rebekah has Esau and Jacob in her womb, God says to her:

Two nations are in your womb, and two peoples from out of your *belly* shall be divided;
the one shall be stronger than the other, the older shall serve the younger. (Gen 25:23, my translation)

Of course, in the father's instance, a child 'coming out of your belly' refers to where the semen comes from, the semen that is the source of life and that is planted in the mother's belly. This is a common biblical way of thinking and talking about how babies are made. Children are seen as being the fruit of the *father's* body (see, for example, Micah 6:7 and Psalm 132:11). And both men and women could be thought of as 'barren' (Deut 7:14).

This very strong biological connection between fathers and their children forged an iron link between a man and his descendants. Fathers were the source of life not only to their own children, but to the generations that followed. An ancient Hebrew looked back to his grandfather or his great-grandfather or even to the greatest-grandfather of them all—Abraham—and simply called him 'father'. His ancestor was the source of his existence. He was the life-giver to his children and all their descendants.

This view is reflected in a curious little verse in the book of Hebrews where the author says:

> One might even say that Levi himself, who receives tithes, paid tithes through Abraham, for he was still in the loins of his ancestor when Melchizedek met him. (Heb 7:9–10)

Never mind the tithes and Melchizedek—notice what is said about Levi and his great-grandfather Abraham. Levi was sort of there when Abraham paid Melchizedek, because he was "still in the loins of his ancestor". Before he was born, before he was even a twinkle in his father Jacob's eye, indeed before Jacob was even a twinkle in his father Isaac's eye—before there were any twinkles in any eyes going back 100 years, the seed that would eventually bear the fruit called 'Levi' was in the loins of Abraham.

Fathers are the source of life to generation after generation of their descendants. They spawn families and clans and tribes. They are life-givers. They are creators.

This is one of the ways in which God himself is described as a father in the Bible—because he is the life-giver, the creator of all.

> Do you thus repay the LORD,
> you foolish and senseless people?
> Is not he your father, who created you,
> who made you and established you? (Deut 32:6)

> "Woe to him who strives with him who formed him,
> a pot among earthen pots!
> Does the clay say to him who forms it, 'What are you making?'
> or 'Your work has no handles'?
> Woe to him who says to a father, 'What are you begetting?'
> or to a woman, 'With what are you in labour?' "
> Thus says the LORD,
> the Holy One of Israel, and the one who formed him:
> "Ask me of things to come;
> will you command me concerning my children and the
> work of my hands?
> I made the earth and created man on it;
> it was my hands that stretched out the heavens,
> and I commanded all their host." (Isa 45:9-12)

God created and gave life to mankind, and in that general sense is the 'father' of all. All of humanity are God's children, because he created and formed us, and gave life to each one of us. (That's not to say, of course, that we are all God's children in the full sense—because we've all rejected him, rebelled against him and run away from home. We're God's estranged children. And if we're ever going to be accepted back into God's family, there's some serious mending of fences to be done, which is why Jesus Christ came into the world to die on a cross—but that's another story.)

Whether it's God's fatherhood, or human fatherhood, the Bible is fairly clear. In the biblical way of viewing the world, fathers are life-givers. In biblical families, fathers were not junior partners. They were not shadowy, uninvolved figures drifting on the edges. *They were at the centre.* As one biblical scholar describes it: "Like the spokes of a wheel, family life radiated out from him".[1]

Our trouble is that hardly anybody thinks this now. In modern families, perhaps the most we hope for is that dad will at least pull his weight; that he will make an effort to take an interest, be home for dinner, and maybe go to the occasional athletics carnival. We hope that he will be involved, that he will at least do his share. But it never occurs to us to put the father at the *centre* of the family life. If anyone is at the centre, it is mum. She is the one who holds the family together. She's the rock on which it's all built, who organizes everything, worries about everything, cares for everyone, sustains everyone. Or perhaps, if we have a truly egalitarian marriage, there is no centre, but two equal points around which the family revolves in orbit. Or, as is too often the case, we are simply a loose collective of individuals with no centre at all.

I don't wish to run down motherhood (my best friend is a mother). Nor do I want to suggest for a minute that the baby-making business is anything other than a partnership. What I want to do is change the way you think about the father's place in that partnership. The Bible's model of fatherhood has dad as the senior partner, the initiator, the planter of the seed.

Here is the first point at which I want to change what's going on between your ears. If you're a father—and I'm assuming that most readers of this book are—I want you to stop and think about your children. Which of the words from the following list would you choose to describe your relationship with them? Are you their:

- protector?
- friend?
- cash-cow?
- master?
- servant?
- chauffeur?
- provider?
- hero?
- long-lost relative?

- counsellor?
- teacher?
- judge?
- Mr Fixit?
- object of ridicule?

Depending on which day it is, I could tick any one of those. But the word that should be at the top of that list is: *creator*. You made your children. You gave them life. They are the fruit of your own body.

God, of course, is the capital 'C' Creator, but his way of doing things is usually to work through his creation. He works through us as fathers to create new life.

I don't know whether you ever have those moments when the reality of being a father smacks you between the eyes. It sometimes happens to me when we've all piled into the people-carrier to go somewhere. I turn around from the driver's seat and there are faces staring back at me. Five of them. It seems only yesterday that Ali and I were driving a red Mini, and there was nothing in the back seat at all except maybe a very 1980s khaki bomber-jacket, which was fine because it was 1985 at the time.

But now there are three rows of seats and five little (or not so little any more) bodies where the bomber-jacket used to be. "How on earth did they get there?" I think to myself.

The answer is: I put them there. I created those five little lives. I planted them. Ali bore them. And there they are, joking and squabbling and wondering why I'm staring at them with a philosophical look on my face instead of starting the car.

The first revolution in a father's thinking is the recognition that his children are the fruit of his own body. He made them. He gave them life. They are his.

As we shall soon see, everything flows from this.

ENDNOTE
1. D. L. Bock, 'Marriage and family in Ancient Israel' in K. M. Campbell (ed), *Marriage and Family in the Biblical World*, IVP, Downers Grove, 2003, p. 43.

CHAPTER 3
A RIVER TO HIS PEOPLE

FATHERS MIGHT BE feeling rather bullish after chapter 2. Poor cousins in the baby-creating business no longer! I planted the seed. I gave him life. That's *my* boy playing out there in the garden.

Before we get too carried away with our newfound importance, it might be worth thinking about the consequences. If fathers are the life-givers, the senior partners in the creation of children, then it follows that we are ultimately *responsible* for the lives that we have initiated and brought into being.

What you create belongs to you.

This book, for example, is mine. I created every word in it. If anyone tries to copy it, steal it or otherwise rip it off, I won't be too happy (in fact, I'd probably have a whinge to my lawyer). If it becomes a worldwide bestseller, I will gratefully enjoy the satisfaction that such an unlikely event would bring. If it helps vast numbers of men do better as fathers, then I will rejoice at having been used by God to achieve such a worthy end. But if, on the other hand, it's a dreadful flop, then it's really no-one's fault but mine. If it confuses and hinders dads from being what God wants them to be, it will be on my own head. And if I libel someone, it will be me that gets sued, my house that gets sold, and my kids that abuse me for having cost them all any chance of a DVD player.

Our kids are the books we write. The glory we receive when they become bestsellers is rightfully ours. But so is the responsibility we have for them. This is why our wives might be smiling after chapter 2. Could it be (they wonder to themselves) that he is actually going to take *responsibility*?

Certainly, when we turn back to the Bible, and to what fatherhood looks like, this is a common idea. Fathers, in the biblical world, had a natural responsibility to care for their children, to nourish them, to provide for them, to seek their welfare, and in the end to give them an inheritance. The father was the one who had generated the life of the family, who had brought forth children as the fruit of his body. And so the father was ultimately responsible for them.

This is reflected in the biblical phrase that most closely resembles our modern word 'family'—the *father's house*. If you lived in ancient Israel, you didn't speak about your 'family' but about your 'father's house'. Of the many references to this idea, here's an interesting one from Genesis 31. Jacob has nicked off during the night from his

Uncle Laban's, taking Laban's daughters Rachel and Leah with him. Laban is none too pleased about this, especially because his 'household gods' are also missing—that is, the little gold idols that he worships. When he catches up with Jacob, Laban says to him:

> "And now you have gone away because you longed greatly for your father's house, but why did you steal my gods?" (Gen 31:30)

When we think of 'longing for our father's house', we might think of going home on holidays to Mum and Dad's, and spending a few days in the old place again. Or perhaps we might long for Mum and Dad to kick the bucket so that we can inherit it! But this wasn't what Laban was talking about. Jacob's father Isaac was already long dead, and he didn't have a house anyway—they were nomads who lived in tents. Jacob 'longing for his father's house' simply meant that he wanted to be back with his family and relatives. That's what his 'father's house' was— it was all those who had been given life by his father, and who were part of the household that his father had created. And he continued to belong to that 'house' even after his father's death.

This very strong connection between a father and his children was symbolized in a moving ceremony called the 'redemption of the firstborn'. As part of their celebration of the Exodus from Egypt, Israelites were to give their firstborn sons to God, and then to buy them back (to 'redeem' them, as you would a watch that you had traded for cash at the pawnbrokers). And when their sons asked what this was all about, they were to say:

> "By strength of hand the LORD brought us out of Egypt, from the house of slavery. For when Pharaoh stubbornly refused to let us go, the LORD killed all the firstborn in the land of Egypt, both the firstborn of man and the firstborn of animals. Therefore I sacrifice to the LORD all the males that first open the womb, but all the first-born of my sons I redeem." (Exod 13:14–15)

At the redemption of the firstborn, the father was saying to his son, "You are a gift to me from the Lord, and I want to keep you. I will buy you back, as the Lord redeemed us from Egypt. You will be part of my house, and I will care and provide for you, and I will give you an inheritance— as the Lord has given one to us."

It's sometimes suggested that in the ancient world, and in Israel as much as elsewhere, fathers regarded children merely as their property, to do with as they pleased. There is some truth in this. In extreme poverty, Israelite fathers were reduced to selling their children into slavery, so as to save both children and parents from starvation. And this could hardly be done if the father was not regarded as the child's 'owner'.

But as the 'redemption of the firstborn' shows, Israelite fathers 'owned' their children in the way that we sometimes use the word today. They had a total commitment to them. They regarded them as the blessing of God, to be loved and nurtured. And in this, Israel was markedly different from the nations around them. They did not sacrifice their children to appease the gods (as the nations around them did). They did not kill unwanted children (as the nations around them did). They treasured their children, as an extraordinary blessing from God. As the psalmist sang:

> Behold, children are a heritage from the LORD,
> the fruit of the womb (lit. *belly*) a reward.
> Like arrows in the hand of a warrior
> are the children of one's youth.
> Blessed is the man
> who fills his quiver with them!
> He shall not be put to shame
> when he speaks with his enemies in the gate. (Ps 127:3-5)

We don't tend to think about kids this way. Perhaps we would write the psalm like this:

> Behold, children are just a nuisance,
> the fruit of the womb a pain in the neck.
> Like arrows in the backside of a warrior
> are the children of one's youth.
> Blessed is the man
> who can persuade his wife to stop at two.

He shall not be put to shame
when his mates invite him to the pub.

To the fathers of biblical times, the idea of *wanting* to stop at two would have been hard to understand. To their minds, children were a gift or reward from God, and the more the better. This was clearly because children were not just gifts and responsibilities and burdens; they were arrows in the hand of a warrior. They were his, the 'fruit of the belly' (whether his own belly or that of his wife the psalm doesn't specify). How glad he was to have them.

One of my favourite scenes in *Lawrence of Arabia* is the speech by Anthony Quinn as the Arab tribal chief Auda abu Tayi, after Lawrence has just suggested that Auda is but a servant of the Turks. Auda stands with a look of indignation on his face and says: "I carry 23 great wounds all got in battle. 75 men have I killed with my own hands in battle. I scatter. I burn my enemies' tents. I take away their flocks and herds. The Turks pay me a golden treasure, yet I am poor—*because I am a river to my people*". I've tried the same line on my tribe as we've sat around a wooden park bench on the promenade of Coogee Beach, a feast of fish and chips spread out before us (oh yes and some McNuggets because there are two who don't like fish), the salty tang of the sea-breeze in our nostrils, cups of fizzy drink in our hands. "I am poor—because I am a river to my people", I bellow, in my best Anthony Quinn voice. They look at me and roll their eyes, except one of those who doesn't like fish, who punches me in the arm.

The father as provider. It feels like an old-fashioned idea, but there's a deep truth in it. Our children are our own creation, under God. We made them. They come from our own bodies. And so we're responsible to care for them, to provide for them, to love them.

We see this in the Scripture as 'father' becomes another word for 'provider'. When Job describes himself as "a father to the needy" (Job 29:16), he means that he was their protector and provider. They had no-one else, and so he stepped in and took up their cause. He gave them what they needed; he supported them, fed them, housed them, and sought justice for them. He was a father to them.

Joseph is saying much the same thing when he says that God "has made me a father to Pharaoh" (Gen 45:8). It is to Joseph that Pharaoh turned in his hour of need, to get Egypt through its years of famine. Joseph became the one who provided food for a whole nation, and indeed for his own family as they came down to Egypt to look for provisions. He was being a 'father'.

That is why there is perhaps no sadder state to be in, Bible-wise, than to be fatherless. It puts you in the company of the widows, the weak, the oppressed, the refugees, the poor—all those who are victimized and oppressed by the rich and powerful of society. God, however, is the "father of the fatherless", as Psalm 68:5 puts it. He watches out for the orphans, and protects the widows. He's a father to them.

In fact, the Bible's picture of God as a father is a perfect one for we earthly fathers to imitate. God is the ultimate father, who cares for and sustains and nurtures his creation.

> The eyes of all look to you,
> and you give them their food in due season.
> You open your hand;
> you satisfy the desire of every living thing. (Ps 145:15-16)

God is a faithful father to what he has made. He supervises and sustains and provides for all his creation. He makes his sun rise on both the evil and the good, and sends rain on the just and the unjust alike (Matt 5:45).

In the same way, the human father's role is to provide generously and lovingly for his family, because he is responsible for them. He has given them life; it is his job to sustain and nurture that life.

All this seems blindingly obvious. Of course it's our job as fathers to look after our families. What sort of man would dodge this responsibility?

Answer: plenty of men.

The obligation fathers have to protect and provide for their own children may be intuitively obvious, morally unquestionable and socially supported—but that doesn't stop countless men in our culture absolving themselves of it. Some simply run away. Others remain within the family home, but fail to take their responsibility seriously. They leave their wives or partners to worry about the kids and to provide for their needs. They are the present-but-absent fathers, for whom family life is an unwelcome interruption to their other activities—whether that be pursuing their career or socializing or playing sport.

I don't think it's an accident that the appalling lack of responsibility shown by many fathers for their children has grown in a culture where the role and place of the father in creating children has been reduced to the point of non-existence. In our society, the child is a subset of the mother. It is part of her body, such that she may dispose of it if she wishes. It is the mother who creates the child, who 'owns' the child, and who therefore bears chief responsibility for the child.

I think most of us (men, that is) have learnt to think this way, almost without realizing it. And it eats away at the sense of responsibility we should have towards our children.

This is what's so attractive about the Bible's view of fatherhood. It doesn't diminish the (very obvious) role of the mother or separate her from the care and nurture of her children. That would hardly be possible. But the Bible brings the father from the outskirts right into the centre.

The child is the fruit of *his* body. He gave it life, and so he is *responsible* for that life.

This is not a responsibility the father takes up unwillingly or begrudgingly. In the Bible, fathers long to give good things to their children:

> Which one of you, if his son asks him for bread, will give him a stone? Or if he asks for a fish, will give him a serpent? If you then, who are evil, know how to give good gifts to your children, how much more will your Father who is in heaven give good things to those who ask him! (Matt 7:9-11)

This is a picture of fatherhood that's hard not to like: the father as a generous, open-handed provider; a fierce and diligent protector; a loving nurturer and giver of good gifts. Many of us no doubt wish we had fathers like that. There's not much we can do about it if we didn't. What we *can* do is assume responsibility for our own children.

In practice

If we're going to take *responsibility* for our families, for their care and nurture and growth, what's it going to mean in practice? Well, a thousand things—from how we choose to spend our Saturday mornings, to what decisions we make about education. I don't want to limit your imagination in working out how to put the principles into practice.

However, here are five suggestions to get you started.

1. *Never leave*

I would be surprised if there was not a father reading this book who has not, at some dark and desperate hour, thought within the quiet rooms of his own heart, "This is not what I signed up for. What sort of life is this? I'm 45, I've worked my guts out, and what am I getting for it? Aggravation, criticism, and hardly a spare minute to do anything that I feel like doing. Besides which I'm just bored out of my brain. Well, I'm out of here."

The temptation simply to leave, to run away from it all, can be strong. You may even justify these feelings by considering your own failings and inadequacies—"They'd probably be better off without me anyway, since I can't seem to do anything right".

But you can no more escape your responsibility for the lives you have brought into being than escape your own desire for survival. They are yours. They belong to you, and you to them. You may not be able to nurture them as well as you would like, or provide for them as richly as you would like, but one thing every father can do is *never leave*. Your place is with them, like a captain with his troops. They need you. And you have a responsibility to care for them which you will answer for to the face of God. To cut and run when the battle is at its height is not just an evasion of that grave responsibility. In the end, it's cowardice.

2. Don't act the hero when you're just doing your job

Here's a test to see whether you've absorbed the mind-change contained in this chapter. Say you've just done something good for your family—you might have decided to take care of dinner on Saturday night to give your wife a break; or you take the whole family out to the beach late on Sunday afternoon for some games and fish and chips; or you call everyone together for a family prayer time after dinner. When you do something like this, do you have that warm glow of smug satisfaction? Do you fish for a compliment from your wife? Is the voice in your head saying: "Look, I've just gone way Above and Beyond the Call of Duty. At least half of all this stuff is really her job, and here am I doing it for her. Am I a hero or what?"

The fact is, you're just doing what you're supposed to do. You're just fulfilling your responsibility to care for, nourish, love and provide for your family—to give of yourself for their wellbeing. The responsibility is not divided in half—or as is too often the case 60/40 or 70/30 with the wife taking up most of the slack. The responsibility is yours. 100%. Of course, you'll divide up the jobs and day-to-day responsibilities with your wife, but in the end the buck stops with you. If you do something great for your family, it's fine to feel good about it. You've done what you should be doing. But don't act as if you've done *more* than you should be doing.

3. Talking good, mind-reading bad

There are few things more infuriating for husbands than when your wife won't tell you what the problem is, and you're just supposed to know. In the end, you look blankly at her and say, "Well no, I don't know what the problem is. Can you just tell me?" And then you not only get in trouble for whatever the problem is, but also for being such a blind, deaf, insensitive brute as not to *realize* what the problem is.

But the lack of clear talk and communication can be just as much a problem from our side. Why wait until there's a problem? Shouldn't we be talking with our wives regularly about how things are going, not only in her life, but in the life of the family? If, a week earlier, we'd taken an hour over coffee just to chat about life and how things were going, the problem might have been aired and dealt with before it became a bone of contention.

Many males are not natural chatterers. That's OK—we don't have to be. We just have to be loving and interested enough to ask the question, to listen, to talk things through, to work things out. Make sure you're taking the initiative to talk to your wife, and to *listen* to your wife. It will save you having to mind-read later on.

4. Try to be an all-rounder

Some dads provide everything materially and physically that their kids will ever need, but leave them so emotionally starved that they grow up as stunted, malformed personalities. Some dads look after their family's physical needs, and their human needs for relationship and emotional security, but provide no spiritual or moral sustenance—and the kids grow up without purpose, character or a vital relationship with God.

We need to keep providing for the whole range of needs that our families have, and not neglecting any of them. One helpful way to think about this is to think of your kids as having three bank accounts: one each for their physical, emotional and spiritual needs (if I can summarize them like that). You can think of your role as a dad as making sure that something is being banked in each of these accounts on a regular basis.

- Physically—are they getting exercise, eating well, sleeping well?
- Emotionally—do you spend time with them? Do they have friends?
- Spiritually—how are they being taught and encouraged in the Lord?

Have a think about your own performance as father in

relation to each of your children. For each child, which of the three accounts has the lowest balance? Which the highest? Where do you need to make some changes?

We'll come back to look at the third of those bank accounts in more detail in Part II of this book.

5. Quality of intake

The final practical suggestion follows on from the previous one. We should not only make sure that our kids are being fed in the different areas of life, but that what they're taking in is of good quality. In particular, we need to take responsibility for what our children are reading and watching, because this will effect their intellectual, emotional and spiritual growth in all sorts of ways.

This is a struggle for most parents. Who hasn't had their 10-year-old plead with them to see the entirely inappropriate 15-rated movie that 'everyone else in the class has seen'? And to make life more complex, different Christian parents will make different decisions on what is or is not suitable for their kids to watch or read.

This is not an area for legislation, but here are some tips I've gleaned from experience and from talking to others:

• Make it clear to your kids that decisions about movies, TV shows and books are your responsibility, just as the quality of food they eat is your responsibility. I sometimes explain it to my kids like this: "God has given us the job of feeding you and looking after you until you're old enough to do it yourself. Kids don't always know what the best thing to eat is: if I left it up to you, you'd probably eat nothing but chocolate and chips all day, which wouldn't be good for you. It's the same with movies and TV. We've got to make sure that what you're feeding into your brain is good food, and won't hurt you, especially if you eat too much of it. When you're old enough, you'll be able to make your own decisions about what to watch (and eat), but in the meantime it's our job to look after you. You won't always agree with what we decide, but there's only one reason we'll ever stop you from watching something: if we think it will be harmful to you."

- Have some simple rules of thumb that prevent you from having to decide everything case-by-case. In our house, the rule for movies is: No-one under the age of 15 watches 15-rated movies, unless Mum and Dad decide to make a special exception (having seen the film and been satisfied it's OK).

- If a child is desperate to watch a particular TV show or film that, for example, teaches an ungodly view of the world or promotes ungodliness, another option is to watch it together and talk about it afterwards. This is a great way to teach your kids to process the messages that the world sends, and to respond to them as Christians.

- Try to be positive and proactive rather than only ever saying, "You can't watch that". Take your kids to the movies. Sit down and laugh together at a TV comedy. Read a book around the table after dinner. Send them the message that culture is a good thing, to be enjoyed with thanksgiving as God's gift.

All of this requires us not only to take responsibility, but to make decisions for the welfare of our children. And this leads us to the subject of our next chapter.

CHAPTER 4

THE POWER TO SERVE

Used by permission

THIS IS ONE OF the nightmares of working life—where we are held accountable for something over which we have no real control or authority. We're given a deadline and a budget, but the budget is so miserly that there is no way we can meet the deadline and have a quality result at the same time.

Or we're told that a particular project is 'our baby', and that we can run with it. But our boss ends up vetting every decision, and over-ruling us at key points. And when the whole thing falls over it's still seen as our fault.

Where there is responsibility, but not the resources or authority to meet that responsibility, frustration is the inevitable result. It's not right. If you're going to be called to account for something, then you ought to have the power and authority to do the job, especially in being authorised to make key decisions.

This is one of the latest fads in the always faddish world of business and management thinking. Some genius at the Harvard School of Business (or somewhere) has figured out that if you want a workforce to be efficient, and to be able to effectively execute strategy, then you need to assign 'decision-rights' very carefully and clearly, so that decisions are made once at the appropriate level, rather than being made more than once, at the wrong level, or not at all.

(Hallelujah, you think to yourself. One thing I'd like decision-rights over is the decision to skip the latest management seminar so that I can actually get some work done!)

All the same, responsibility does require authority. And authority brings responsibility. The two cannot be separated.

This brings us to the next major feature of fatherhood. You'll recall that so far we've looked at two big themes. We've seen first of all that fathers are the prime *creators* of their children; they give them life. We've also thought about the *responsibility* that goes along with that creation—how fathers are to be totally committed to their kids, to care for them, to nurture them, to love them.

The third key feature of fatherhood follows on from these first two. Since fathers give life to their children, and are therefore ultimately responsible for them, they must have *authority* in the family, so as to be able to fulfil their responsibility. In the biblical way of thinking, fathers are in charge of their families. They are worthy of honour and obedience from their children. They lead. They have decision-rights.

These days, this a controversial thing to say. The idea of dad being the 'head of the household' is dismissed as a relic from the repressive, chauvinist, hopelessly-outdated world of the past. However, this is about as fair or helpful as regarding all feminists as angry, bra-burning, hairy-legged radicals in boilersuits. (Excellent joke for use in a variety of contexts: "Q. What's the difference between a sabre-toothed tiger and a feminist with a sense of humour? A. One is an extinct species and the other never existed." If you tell this one to a bunch of blokes, it normally goes down well. And if you tell it to some feminists, and receive a cold, icy stare in response—well, you've proved your point.)

Perhaps 'controversial' is the wrong word to describe the idea that fathers have authority in their households. It may have been controversial in the 1960s and 70s, but for most people now, in the 21st century, it's simply not on the agenda. It is more likely to be regarded as just crazy, or even quaint. To suggest it as a serious option is to declare yourself as coming from another planet.

However, we need to remember that in thinking this

way, our culture is out on its own at the end of a long and lonely limb. Perched on our branch, we have Western society, which for about 25 years has widely accepted the notion that men and women are not just equal in dignity and rights, but identical in pretty much every respect (except those respects in which women are clearly superior). The idea of husbands and fathers having a central and authoritative role in the family has been decried, derided and destroyed. And has the result been an explosion in family happiness, togetherness and harmony? Hardly.

The rest of the gigantic oak tree to which we are attached, with a massive trunk and branches too numerous to count, represents thousands of years of human history and culture, not just in the West but all over the world. And on every one of those innumerable branches is a culture that has recognized that despite our fundamental unity, husbands and wives are irreducibly diverse; that there are different roles and functions appropriate to each; and that husbands and fathers should be at the centre of family life, with some measure of authority.

To argue for the authority of fathers is to argue for the historically normal position, the one that has characterized human family relationships almost universally throughout history—except for that somewhat novel experiment called the feminist revolution in the last quarter of the twentieth century in Western society. We need to remind ourselves that it's the modern feminist West that is decidedly odd on this question.

However, going with what the majority of families in world history have done is no reason to do something, even if it might reassure us that we're not from another planet. We need a clear explanation not only of *why* fathers have authority, but exactly *what* that authority means in practical terms.

Let's start by dispelling some myths:

- The authority of fathers is *not* based on superior physical strength or expressed by physical dominance. Some forms of authority in our world are based on might and force of arms—such as the authority of the government to lock us up if we choose to disobey. Fatherly authority does not stem from this, nor should it be expressed like this.

- It is *not* based on superiority of mind or soul. Fathers do not derive their authority on account of being a higher class of human being than mothers, either intellectually or morally. Most of us need very little convincing of this. If there is any form of superiority that fathers have, it is a superiority of responsibility and commitment (as we saw in our last chapter).

- A father's authority is *not* arbitrary or random—as if in the beginning God flipped a coin to see who would wear the pants, and the winner (or should that be loser?) was the father. There is a reason for his authority, and it has to do with his role as the prime generator of the family's life, and the one who is ultimately responsible to sustain and nurture that life.

- Nor is a father's authority solitary. He exercises it in partnership with his wife. In the Bible, fathers are unquestionably seen as the heads of households—and yet the commandment also says, "Honour your father and mother" (Exod 20:12). Mothers as well as fathers exercise this authority within the household. Like fathers, they teach and instruct their children (see Prov 1:8; 6:20). Whatever a father's authority is, it is not the lordly rule of a high king, seated on his solitary throne with his subjects grovelling at his feet. At the very least, there is a queen sitting beside him.

- A father's authority has *no necessary connection* with the humiliation of women or their oppression. It is not an authority against his wife. It is for her benefit—to serve and please her, to seek her welfare, to direct the family's affairs for her advantage.

- Likewise, the authority of a father is *not* directed towards crushing his children or turning them into slaves. It is not an exercise in power for its own sake. On the contrary, a father's authority is directly related to his responsibility for his family. A father's authority is not aimed at securing his own wellbeing, comfort, security, pleasure or happiness. He does not rule in order to gather benefits for himself, ordering his subjects to serve him and to satisfy his wishes.

When we turn to the Bible on this question, we don't find any passages that explicitly mount an argument as to *why* a father should have authority in his family—as if it were a controversial idea that needed to be defended. In passages all over the Bible, it is simply assumed to be the case, as it has been in most cultures for most of human history. Here is a brief selection of biblical examples:

- In Malachi 1:6, God says to Israel, "A son honours his father, and a servant his master. If then I am a father, where is my honour?" The implication is clear: sons honour fathers. That's how it should be, because fathers have rightful authority in the household.

- Ephesians 6:1 says that children should obey their parents in the Lord, "for this is right". Simple as that. It's just the way the world is created to be, and that's presumably why Paul goes on to say: "Honour your father and mother (this is the first commandment with a promise) that it may go well with you and that you may live long in the land".

- In Hebrews 12:7, in talking about the discipline that our heavenly Father sends on his children for their good, the author says, "For what son is there whom his father does not discipline?" Since the discipliner always has authority over the 'disciplinee', this is a statement about the normal authority of fathers over their children. (The same implication is found in Ephesians 6:4 where fathers are explicitly commanded to discipline and instruct their children.)

- The book of Proverbs is essentially the words of a father to a son, to teach him the wisdom that is founded on the 'fear of the Lord'. Throughout Proverbs, it is assumed that it is a father's rightful expectation that his son will heed his teaching, and respect his authority. "Listen to your father who gave you life, and do not despise your mother when she is old" it says in Proverbs 23:22. And putting it more negatively: "If one curses his father or his mother, his lamp will be put out in utter darkness" (Prov 20:20).

Now in some of these Bible passages, you may have noticed that mothers get a fairly equal share of the authority. They are to be honoured, obeyed and respected every bit as much as fathers. And this is something that fathers should always insist upon. It's certainly a hot button issue in our family. If I arrive home and Ali has been reduced to a state of angry, tearful frustration from losing the struggle for obedience and cooperation—well, my kids know that it's warpath time. Very few things make me madder, and it's one of those (unfortunately rare) instances where my anger is righteous.

However, does the Bible say that fathers have *ultimate* authority in the family? As a matter of fact it does, and for very interesting reasons. There are three passages we should take some time to look at.

The first two relate to the authority husbands have over wives with respect to teaching and church life:

> Let a woman learn quietly with all submissiveness. I do not permit a woman to teach or to exercise authority over a man; rather, she is to remain quiet. For Adam was formed first, then Eve; and Adam was not deceived, but the woman was deceived and became a transgressor. (1 Tim 2:11-14)

> But I want you to understand that the head of every man is Christ, the head of a wife is her husband, and the head of Christ is God. ... For a man ought not to cover his head, since he is the image and glory of God, but woman is the glory of man. For man was not made from woman, but woman from man. Neither was man created for woman, but woman for man. (1 Cor 11:3, 7-9)

These are controversial and (to us) difficult passages, and we'll leave a discussion of what these passages mean for church life, women's ministry, and all those other subjects for another time. What we need to notice at this point is the *reason* for the authority given to men. Both passages go back to creation and to the way that man and woman first came to be. There's something about the way men and women were first created that gives their relationship a particular order, such that a husband has a measure of authority over his wife. But what is it? Is it that men were created first in time; that they arrived on the scene in advance of the woman, and so get to be in charge? Is there a principle of 'first in, most authority'? It's hard to see how that would be the case, since the creation story makes it clear that the animals, who came before man, are also under the authority of both men and women (see Gen 1:28). If it was just about who happened to get created first, then the plants would rule the animals, and the animals would rule man, and all of them would tell the woman what to do.

The reason is made clear in the 1 Corinthians passage. It's the fact that man did not come from woman, but woman from man. God took one of the man's ribs and formed the woman out of it.

The point that Adam so joyfully proclaims is: "This at last is bone of my bones and flesh of my flesh; she shall be called Woman, because she was taken out of Man" (Gen 2:23). The woman comes out of the man's own body. She is his very own flesh and bones. Her life came from his life. And it is on this basis, says Corinthians, that she is his glory, and that he is her head.[2]

This fits with what we have been suggesting about the

connection between the authority of the father and his generation of the life of his family. He is the source of the family's life—his children spring from his own body—and so he is both responsible for that life, and has authority over it. This seems to be Paul's argument as well: the fact that Adam gave rise to Eve, that she was taken out of his body, means that he has a certain responsibility for her, and a certain authority over her.

Now the nature of this authority is explained in more detail in the third passage we should look at: the famous one about marriage in Ephesians 5:22–33.

> Wives, submit to your own husbands, as to the Lord. For the husband is the head of the wife even as Christ is the head of the church, his body, and is himself its Saviour. Now as the church submits to Christ, so also wives should submit in everything to their husbands. Husbands, love your wives, as Christ loved the church and gave himself up for her, that he might sanctify her, having cleansed her by the washing of water with the word, so that he might present the church to himself in splendour, without spot or wrinkle or any such thing, that she might be holy and without blemish. In the same way husbands should love their wives as their own bodies. He who loves his wife loves himself. For no one ever hated his own flesh, but nourishes and cherishes it, just as Christ does the church, because we are members of his body. "Therefore a man shall leave his father and mother and hold fast to his wife, and the two shall

become one flesh." This mystery is profound, and I am saying that it refers to Christ and the church. However, let each one of you love his wife as himself, and let the wife see that she respects her husband.

The basic point here is that wives and husbands are united as one body, just as Christ and the church are, with Christ/husbands as the head, and the church/wives as the body. The role of husbands is to love, protect and nourish their own bodies—that is, their wives—just as Christ has done for his body by laying down his life. It's an authority or headship that is put into practice by loving the other person. It is not a headship or authority that serves itself, or that exists to benefit itself. Its sole purpose is the growth and wellbeing of another—in this case, the wife.

I once heard a marriage sermon from Ephesians 5, in which the preacher said that, according to this passage, husbands were to exercise headship over their wives in three ways: they were to love her (v. 25), they were to love her (v. 28), and they were to love her (v. 33).

That's what the authority of a husband and father is like. It is certainly about being in charge and saying what goes; it's about making decisions and taking the lead. But it's making decisions *for the sake of others*. It's having the authority to decide that your family holiday this summer won't be spent at home fiddling about in the shed and watching the cricket (which is what you'd prefer), but at a quiet little beach-house because you know that would be much more relaxing and refreshing for your wife. It's calling the family together for a Bible-reading and prayer time after the evening meal—even though you're exhausted and just want to sit down, your wife feels the same, and the kids would rather be playing on the computer. It's deciding not to take a promotion at work because you know that the extra hours involved would hurt your marriage and your children.

It's the kind of authority, in other words, that the Son of God himself showed, and which he called on his followers to imitate:

> "You know that those who are considered rulers of the Gentiles lord it over them, and their great ones exercise authority over them. But it shall not be so among you. But whoever would be great among you must be your servant, and whoever would be first among you must be slave of all. For even the Son of Man came not to be served but to serve, and to give his life as a ransom for many." (Mark 10:42-45)

We need to think more about what a father's authority means in practice, but before we do, let's summarize:

What is authority? It's the right and power to make decisions, and thus to call forth action in others, in fulfilment of one's responsibility.

What is the basis of a father's authority? The father is the source of life for his family, and thus has a responsibility and commitment to pursue the wellbeing of his family. He is given authority in the family to fulfil this responsibility.

What is the purpose of a father's authority? A father is given the power to make decisions and to call forth action from family members, not for his own benefit but for the benefit of his wife and children.

Now we need to think more about what this authority means in practice.

ENDNOTE

2. An aside for those who are interested in such things: a scholarly spat has been going on in recent years over the meaning of the Greek word *kephale* translated 'head' in 1 Corinthians 11 and elsewhere. The usual and common meaning of the word is 'head', as in one who has authority over another—as in the English expressions, the 'head' of the maths department or army 'head'-quarters. However, some scholars have argued that *kephale* can also mean 'source'—as in the 'head' of the river—and that nothing is being said in 1 Corinthians about authority, only about source or origin. As far as I can tell, the scholars holding the 'source' argument have been given a bloody nose in the course of the debate. The evidence all flows the other way. However, what interests me is that even if the word *were* to have some connotation of 'source' about it (which it almost certainly doesn't), it would only serve to reinforce the biblical idea of authority rather than deny it—because Paul would then be arguing that the reason for the difference in men's and women's roles (which 1 Corinthians goes on to describe) is that he is the source of the woman's life and existence. She was taken out of man, and thus looks to man for leadership.

CHAPTER 5

PRACTICAL AUTHORITY

WHEN I GO TO men's conventions or seminars on fatherhood, and hear all this stirring stuff about authority and decision-making and being the strong leader that our family needs, I find that it sometimes has a curiously deadening effect. I nod, and blankly acknowledge that it's all true. I feel quite sure that whatever the speaker is talking about, I'm almost certainly not doing it very well, if at all. I feel some guilt, and a sense of frustration. But somehow, I have difficulty translating it into action, of knowing what it means *in practice* to lead my family, to be in charge, to exercise authority.

That's what I want to talk about in this chapter: what does it mean *in practice* to be an authoritative leader in your family? If you're convinced in principle that fathers should be exercising authority, but you just aren't quite sure how, then read on. (And if you're not convinced in principle, it might still be worth reading on to see how the model I'm proposing is expressed in action.)

We'll look at it under two headings:

- How do fathers express their authority?
- How should their authority be received?

1. How do fathers express their authority?

I think this question has at least four answers.

(i) In love

We've already mentioned this but it's worth fleshing out: fathers express their authority *in love*. The kind of authority or leadership that fathers are to show has nothing to do with the bossy, selfish brute of a father who wields power so as to please himself, make his life comfortable, and oppress his wife and children. This cartoon-style bad-guy is often presented as an argument against fathers having authority in the family. However, it is not an argument at all but a description of the poor behaviour of some fathers. It is certainly true that some fathers behave like this, just as it is true some mothers are selfish, manipulative shrews who emotionally destroy their husbands and torment their children. But the existence of brutish fathers does not make fatherly authority a bad idea, any more than the existence of awful mothers makes motherly partnership a bad idea. Should we argue, on the basis that some mothers are nasty pieces of work, that all mothers should remain silent, and be kept in a state of strictly controlled oppression? That would be ridiculous, but that is the level of argument that is sometimes wielded against the idea of fatherly authority.

Remember, a father's authority is given to him for one

overriding purpose: so that he can pursue the wellbeing of his family. Since he is ultimately responsible and accountable for his family, he needs the power to fulfil this responsibility. The decisions he makes, and the initiatives he undertakes, will be directed to this end. What this means is that fathers will keep sacrificing their own interests and desires for the sake of their families.

Here's a real-life example with the details changed: James has been married for 15 years, has three kids aged 7-13, and runs his own small business. Life is fast and furious on all fronts, and James realizes that he and his wife Julie just don't spend much time together at all anymore—because there isn't any time. Saturdays are full of sport and shopping. Sundays are church. And then you start all over again on Monday morning. James realises that if he doesn't do something about it, and they keep going this way for the next five years, the good relationship he has with his wife will gradually wither and die. And so he talks it over with Julie, and they work out that if James were to work back late on Tuesday nights to get some paper-work done, he could take Wednesday mornings off to spend a few hours with Julie— just to go for a walk, have a coffee, go to the movies, or whatever ('whatever' here being code for rekindling their fast diminishing sex life).

This is a good illustration of a father's authority in action. The whole thing is a bit of a hassle for James—he doesn't really like the late night on Tuesday, and he feels a bit uneasy not being at work on Wednesday mornings. He's worried that it might affect the performance of his business. But he makes the decision to do this for the sake of his wife and their relationship. He ranks his own wishes and desires *below* the wellbeing of his wife, and takes the lead in putting that into practice.

Here's another trivial everyday example: Bill loves his televised sport. He can happily watch the footie, the Rugby (league or union), the motor racing, the cricket, the tennis, you name it. He's even been known to enjoy the bowling internationals (because it's the only thing that's on). Bill remembers his own dad having supreme and absolute control over the TV. He was deaf to the pleas of his kids to watch the latest soap or quiz show. If the News was on, that was it. The remote control was his sole possession—although in those days the remote control was a much simpler device and less likely to get lost under the armchair. It consisted of Bill's dad saying, "Turn it up will you, Bill".

And so, by nature, inclination and family history, Bill tends to think of the TV as his own personal wide world of sports. But what does he do when his teenage daughters want to watch the latest reality TV show about a beautiful girl who has to live for three months in a cottage with seven singing dwarfs who have to audition each week to avoid being evicted? And it happens to coincide with one of his favourite weekly programs, *The Hurling Show*, featuring interviews, results and crazy stunts from the stars of Ireland's favourite sport? And the video's on the blink so that neither of them can at least be taped?

It's a tough call, and I wouldn't like to lay down the law on this one. But it just might enter Bill's head that yes, he does have the right to make decisions about who uses the TV. And that in this instance, his decision will be to forgo the delights of Irish hurling for the sake of his daughters. Perhaps an even better decision would be to turn off the TV for the evening and play cards instead. But that's another issue altogether.

We could multiply examples and scenarios, but the point, I hope, is clear. A father's authority is not for himself. It is for his family. It's expressed in love.

(ii) By making good decisions when he needs to
The second way a father expresses his authority is in making decisions. This seems like a staggeringly obvious thing to say, but it's worth looking at more closely. Nearly all forms of authority are expressed in making decisions, in having 'decision-rights' (as modern management-speak puts it). Your ability to direct the action of others, for example as the foreman on a building site, depends on your ability to make decisions that are binding on your

workers: "We're going to dig the trenches for the footings today—get to it".

But how does this work out in families? Does dad have to sign off on every decision that is made in family life? Does he determine the brand of laundry detergent as well as which school the kids go to? Is he under any obligation to consult his wife and children? Given that there are a thousand decisions, big and small, every day in family life—from whether little Jason will play cricket on Saturdays this term through to where we should live— how is a dad's decision-making authority expressed?

The answer is: *a father needs to make as many decisions as are necessary for him to fulfil his responsibility for the well-being of his family.*

It's a bit like being the CEO of a business (but without the obscenely high pay). Ultimately, you're accountable for whether the business succeeds or fails. You're responsible for delivering the results that the Board of Directors requires. And you have a team working with you, under your leadership, to achieve those results.

Now, a boss who insists on making every decision— from the kind of paper the letterhead is printed on to the formatting of the office memos—is a nightmare to work with and is almost guaranteed to be a failure. That level of 'micro-management' drives everybody mad, saps morale and distracts the CEO from putting proper time into important strategic decisions he should be making. The micro-managing CEO is on a power trip—he so much loves being in control and having the final say that he can't bear to let any aspect of the operation go.

What's more, a CEO will also fail who simply decrees what the company direction will be, without working it through with his senior management, and consulting extensively with his whole team. He won't have his people with him. They might follow his decisions grudgingly and under compulsion, but he won't have their loyalty or their enthusiasm. They won't go the extra yard for him, let alone the extra mile. The best kind of CEO takes his whole team with him. He recognizes that other people have brains, and that he won't always have the best idea. He goes to the trouble of involving his people in the whole process so that they *own* the direction of the business, and *want* to make it work. In fact, the more it feels like a joint team decision, rather than a decree from on high, the more likely it will be to succeed.

That's just good leadership. And that's the way decision-making should happen in families:

- Only make the decision if it's important that you do so (don't exasperate your wife and kids by making them defer every little detail to you for a ruling!).
- Decide to let others make the decision wherever possible—whether it's choosing which movie to see

or picking between three good options for a holiday. Teach your kids to make good decisions by giving them the power to do so, and then allowing them to experience the consequences of their decision, even if the consequences are painful.

- Where possible, work for consensus. If all those involved can agree on the way forward (including yourself), whether it's about the family holiday destination or choices about schooling, then that has to be the best way to make the decision (unless there's no time for lengthy negotiation!).

- Where you need to make the call, do it after as much discussion as possible. Let everyone have a chance to put their point of view, think carefully and pray, and if consensus can't be reached, explain your decision, and do it.

- Here's a biggie for many blokes: don't assume your wife is always right, and don't make decisions simply to please her. It's easy to keep the peace in a household just by doing whatever your wife wants, and most of the time it will be the right thing to do. But don't assume that it always is. And if, after talking about something, you think that her best interests, and the family's, are served by making a different decision, don't be afraid to say so, and to follow through on it.[3]

(iii) By taking the initiative

The third way a father expresses his authority is through showing initiative. This is one that I struggle with, and I suspect I'm not alone!

I find that the demands on my time and energy as a father, and as a worker, are high. Just keeping all the balls in the air and getting through each week seems hard enough. The result of this relentless pressure, for me anyway, is often that I become entirely *reactive* to what's happening on the home front, and rarely proactive. If something's broken, I'll do my best to fix it. If there's a need, I'll try to meet it. If my wife is suggesting it's really time we did this or that, I'll usually go along. Otherwise, I keep my head down and try to be left alone.

However, if I were to translate this kind of attitude to the work environment, I know I'd be in trouble. A thousand desk-calendar clichés come to mind: "So busy fighting off the crocodiles that you never drain the swamp"; "Take time to sharpen the saw, and you'll cut more effectively"; and so on. In any other field of life, we know that it's true—simply to react to each problem that confronts you, and never to think and plan ahead, is a hopeless way of operating. But it's how a great many of us do our fathering.

When was the last time you did any planning as a father? When did you last sit down and think about how things are going in the family—the quality of the relation-ships, the particular issues or problems different kids might have, the long-term financial needs, the spiritual growth or lack of it, and so on—and having thought about it, worked out some goals to aim at, and a plan of action that might get you there?

This can go as far as you want to take it. On a small scale, try getting into the habit of taking 15 minutes first thing Monday morning to think and pray about some-thing in which you could take the initiative this week to improve family life: it might be buying your wife flowers because you know she's been a bit down; or organizing a family day trip to the beach for Saturday afternoon; or realizing that you haven't spent much time with your youngest son recently and so deciding to take him to the park on Sunday afternoon; or preparing a short family Bible study on a topic that you've been discussing together. It doesn't really matter what it is, large or small. The very activity of taking time to pause, think, pray and then take some action, will help enormously.

If you want to take it a bit further, here's an exercise guaranteed to stun your wife and win you admiration and brownie points galore (not that you want to act the hero!). Suggest that it's time you took stock of how things are going in family life. Find a couple of hours alone where you can talk, and then draw up a piece of paper like this:

	Where are we now?		Where we'd like to be in 12 months	Ideas for getting there	One key thing to do
	Give thanks for...	Needs work & prayer...			
Our marriage (sex life; communication; etc.)					
Our family finances					
Our family's spiritual life					
Our relationship with Child 1					
Our relationship with Child 2					
Our relationship with Child 3					
Relationships between the kids					
Other...					

You can vary the items in the left-hand column as much as you want. You may want to think through where each child is at in terms of Christian growth, and make some individual plans about how to help them grow. Or you may want to think about education, or housing needs, or whatever aspect of life is important to you at present. You don't need to deal with every topic or area every time. The truly significant thing is that you are pausing to take stock of the current situation, to identify the key issues, to set some goals for the future, and then do something about reaching them. It doesn't have to be a 14-page strategic plan. You may end up having one key thing that you want to work on in three important areas—that would probably be enough to keep you occupied. And you might decide that some areas are motoring along reasonably well, and don't need any special attention.

For some of us, a planned systematic approach like this just doesn't gel. It's not us. We like the more free-flowing spontaneous approach. That's fine. So long as the free-flowing spontaneity results in the taking of initiative—not just sitting back and letting it all wash over you, and only stirring yourself to action when something is wrong or when your wife complains loudly enough.

One final simple practical truth: If a father doesn't initiate family prayer and Bible reading time, it usually doesn't happen.

(iv) Discipline and teaching

A fourth way a father's authority is expressed is in the twofold task of discipline and teaching. I say 'twofold task' because discipline and teaching are two aspects of the same activity, which is to raise a child to maturity. The father's core responsibility, as we've seen, is to nurture, protect and nourish the life that he has created, so that the child can reach maturity. He is responsible, then, for forming the life and character of his children—for teaching them about life, and themselves, and God. And he cannot fulfil this responsibility without having the authority to teach and to discipline his children.

In Ephesians 6:4, which is a verse we will return to later in this book, fathers are encouraged to nourish or raise their children in the "training and instruction of the Lord" (NIV). The word translated 'training' is an interesting one; it can mean simply to teach or instruct or train in a certain pattern of behaviour, but it can also mean to 'punish', such as in Luke 23:16 where Pilate thinks Jesus has done nothing worthy of death, and so he says, "I will therefore *punish* and release him".

To train someone in something, and especially to train a child, means not only providing the basic content of what should be done, but also instilling that content through practice and discipline. It means rewarding the student when they do it well, and punishing them in some way when they don't. It's like football training—there's some basic content (the moves, the patterns, the basic skills), plenty of hard, sweaty practice, and then rewards (playing well, being selected for the team, winning the game) and punishments (earning the coach's displeasure, missing out on selection, having to do 20 extra push-ups).

This is a helpful way to think about the thorny subject

of discipline in the family. When you need to punish your children, it should not be to vent your anger and frustration, nor even simply to exact retribution upon them for their sins (although sins do deserve retribution!). It should be to teach them, to train them. It's all but impossible to teach and train children without sometimes punishing them in some way; nor can you punish them without teaching them something. (This is worth thinking about when you punish your kids. You *are* teaching them something. What is it?) It is all one package—teaching, instruction, training, modelling, discipline, encouragement, warning, punishment. And the aim of the package is to nourish and train the child, to raise the child to maturity.

We'll talk more about what it means to raise children in the "training and instruction *of the Lord*" in part 2 of this book, but at this point a few comments more generally on discipline might be useful.

Working out an effective system of discipline within a family is one of the most important and difficult things a father has to do. If there is no system—no expectation of what behaviour will be met with what response—then whatever discipline you do enact will be chaotic, haphazard and have little teaching value. We need to teach our kids the kind of behaviour that is desirable, and then have some form of discipline that backs it up—that trains them in it. The words 'some form' in that last sentence are very important, because there is no single right method of discipline that is right for all families and all children, let alone all ages of children.

In our family, for example, we found that with our first three children (all girls), the sometimes controversial issue of smacking hardly entered the discussion. I can remember holding my eldest daughter's arm by the wrist—she was three—and looking sternly into her face, and giving the back of her hand a little emphatic smack as we talked about some particularly dastardly deed that she'd done. In her case, that was just about the equivalent of tying her to the clothesline and giving her 40 lashes with a whip of cords. She would dissolve into tears of remorse, and nothing further needed to be said. When the two boys came along—numbers four and five in our tribe—let's just say that the rules of engagement were a little different, and a slightly more robust approach was necessary.

Nowadays, with our kids aged between 9 and 16, the era of physical discipline has just about passed (although with the boys, it occasionally resurfaces in the case of particularly heinous crimes). These days, a different set of rewards and punishments are necessary. At the moment, we're operating on a 'three strikes and you're out' system. There's a magnetic thing on the fridge we can write on, and each kid's name is there. Whenever they transgress one of three simple rules, they get a strike. Three strikes and the punishment kicks in—usually involving the withdrawal of computer and/or TV privileges for three days. Good behaviour can result in the rubbing out of an existing strike, and at the end of each month, we wipe the slate clean of any strikes that happen to be there and start again.

At the moment, our three simple rules are:

- do your jobs without complaining;
- don't deliberately provoke someone else; and
- do what mum and dad say first time.

Those are the issues that we want to focus on at the moment. But at other times, it might be different things that are at the forefront of the campaign—say, bad language or rudeness to guests or getting music practices done. The important thing is that the rules of the game are clear, that they aren't too complicated, and that you're a good referee—that is, that you're *consistent*. The whole thing breaks down pretty quickly if you don't follow through on the consequences, and of course if you don't apply them fairly to the different kids.

Now, let me emphasize—this is just *one* way of doing it that we're trying at the moment. It's been reasonably successful, but it has its weaknesses, and we'll no doubt have a different approach in the future. There are plenty of alternatives. I know of a family that has a small whiteboard on the wall, with a blue-and-white chequered border, like a police warning sign, and in big letters inside it says: "Parents now targeting …". And they write whatever the current problem happens to be in the blank space. It could be saying 'thank you', or not mimicking other people, or getting to bed at the agreed time.

One of the weaknesses of our current system is that the punishment doesn't often fit the crime, and it is very desirable for the punishment to fit the crime if you can manage it. I was recently told of a father who was trying to get his teenage son to stop slamming the bedroom door. Despite repeated requests, the slamming continued. And so the father simply unscrewed the door from its hinges, and the boy had to go without a door for a week—a particularly effective punishment for a teenager. Another family I know deals with the perennial problem of kids arguing and fighting with each other in a simple way: they lock the two offenders in the bathroom, not to be released until they have sorted out their differences.

The wise principle here is that the closer the form of punishment or reward relates to the behaviour that it is trying to discourage/encourage, the more effective it is likely to be as a means of teaching. The only trouble is, it's just not always possible—either because of the nature of the 'crime', or because of time or other circumstances. And in those instances, some form of more arbitrary consequence becomes necessary.

The important thing is not that you follow any one method or system. The really important thing is that you think about it, talk to your wife about it, and together come up with a set of expectations and consequences that you feel confident about, and that you can put into practice. Your kids need to know the boundaries, and what will happen when they cross them. And you need to make sure that it happens. If you do this, you will train your children, slowly and surely, to live within those boundaries. And hopefully you'll do it in such a way that living within those boundaries makes sense to them, is satisfying and enjoyable for them, and promotes their growth as human beings.

As I've already mentioned, the 'rewards and punishments' side of training and discipline is just one element in a package that should include instruction, teaching, discussion, problem-solving and your own modelling of the right behaviour—no sense having 'Don't be too hard on each other' as one of your three simple rules if you're always coming down on the kids like a ton of lego bricks (that's a lot of bricks). You should regard having to exercise discipline in the home, in whatever form it takes, as *just one part* of your overall responsibility to teach and train, to instruct and educate, to mould and shape your children into the people God wants them to be.

And here's where we modern men have a problem, largely not of our own making. The current structures of our society work against fathers having time to teach and mould their children. We go off to work; they go off to school. Depending on our circumstances, we might see them for a hectic hour or two before bed, and the weekends fly past in a blur of sport, chores and social engagements. The days are gone when a son would grow up alongside his father, learning a trade from him, learning life-skills from him: how to saddle a horse or grease-and-oil change a car or take a lawnmower to bits and then not be able to put it together again.

I don't want to create a mythical golden age of the past, but I think it is beyond doubt that our current work and family structures do separate fathers from their children more than they did at other times in human history. And it's not just our work practices. The way we organize our leisure time only reinforces the divide. Rather than doing things *with* our children, the social pressure is to take them to a never-ending round of activities (gym, ballet, soccer, music lessons, cricket).

All this makes it hard for fathers to be teachers of their children. In an ideal world, I'd like my kids to be alongside me far more than they are, learning and laughing and working together—so that when I came to teach them the Bible it was the most natural thing in the world. And when I came to discipline them, it was just one small element of a rich and varied relationship.

So much for the ideal world. What progress can we make in the real world?

I think fathers need to be deliberate in maximizing opportunities for being with our kids, and having them do things alongside us. Whatever you're doing—from driving down to the hardware store for some nails, to mowing the lawn, to going to the football—invite your kids to be there at your side, helping out, learning from you, talking with you. It often takes longer this way—that is, with their 'help'—but unless we take steps to involve our kids in what we're doing, as often as we can, the current structures of our culture will tend to keep us apart. We'll become spectators of their lives, or at best taxi-drivers, rather than teachers.

2. How should a father's authority be received?

We won't need to spend too much time considering this, because in one sense the answer is obvious. Just as honour and obedience and respect are due to our heavenly Father because he created all things, and in his faithful goodness sustains all things, so human fathers are also worthy of honour, thanks and obedience from their children. The authority of fathers should be received gratefully, respectfully, and with honour.

Sounds fairly straightforward.

However, in our culture, it doesn't seem so straightforward. With the authority of fathers being regarded as a chauvinistic relic of a by-gone age, respect for fathers has also faded. Think of how many TV ads or sitcoms portray mum as the wise, knowing sensible one who holds things together, and dad as the bumbling, well-meaning incompetent, a kind of big, lovable 12-year-old who drives the car and loves his tools, but is essentially clueless.

Modern readers can find it hard to comprehend the horror that biblical writers express for disrespect to parents. Would anyone in the twentieth century have penned words like these? "The eye that mocks a father and scorns to obey a mother will be picked out by the ravens of the valley and eaten by the vultures" (Prov 30:17). That's a particular nasty fate for a child's eye. First it gets picked out by a big, black, sharp-beaked raven, and then it gets dropped somewhere for a vulture to chew on.

We don't appreciate the profound horror of disrespect and dishonour towards parents, because we do not appreciate the profound position of authority in which parents are placed, fathers in particular. We hate all expressions of authority, and seek to chop them down to size. What is left of the authority of parents in our culture is easily mocked.

American Bible teacher and New Testament Professor Don Carson once said to me about raising his teenagers, "We tolerated no sass. Pretty much everything else was negotiable". I've always remembered his words, partly because it was the only time I had ever heard someone use the word 'sass' in a sentence (it means something like 'impudence' or 'disrespect'). If there is respect for the role of parents, and for their authority, then there's plenty of room for discussion and negotiation.

But what if your kids don't really respect you or honour you? What if they treat you as a bit of a joke? Or as a good buddy that they like having around, but whose word they have no intention of heeding?

That brings us to the subject of a father's style.

Endnote

3. Some readers might respond: "Well that sounds fine, but what if she refuses to go along?" Here's a quick response to a tricky question: 1. The big issue is whether your wife accepts, in principle, your right to make decisions. If she doesn't, there's some hard talking to do, and it's much better to do this talking in advance of any actual controversy over particular decisions. You need to make some time to talk about this *now*. Perhaps you could read the first five chapters of this book together as a starting point for the discussion. You may need to bring someone else into the conversation (your pastor, a trusted friend) to help work through it together. 2. If she does accept your authority in principle, but is finding it hard in this particular instance (because she so violently disagrees with your decision!), then don't be a steamroller. Remind her of the principle that she agrees with (your authority, in the end, to make the call), but assure her that, given her deep unhappiness with the decision, you're going to pray more about it, think more about it, talk to a friend about it (to get another perspective), and then talk again with her. You might suggest she does likewise. If after all that, she still refuses to cooperate with your decision, you may need to go back to point 1.

CHAPTER 6
THE CAPTAIN AND
THE NICE-GUY

ALL FATHERS HAVE a personal style, a particular way of doing things.

My own father's style was fairly typical of his generation, judging by what other men my age have told me—that is, a father who regarded his actions as more significant than his words, which were few; who expressed his love for his family through tireless, selfless toil; who didn't have much to do with domestic chores or child-raising apart from a few clearly defined tasks (clearing the table after dinner, washing up); and who would have considered running off with another woman as an utterly low and cowardly act beyond contempt. He was physically and emotionally strong; a loyal, hard-working, no-nonsense man whom I only ever saw cry once. I can't remember him playing with us much, apart from occasionally joining in our fiercely competitive backyard cricket games. And as we got older, he presided over epic games of rummy in the kitchen around the formica table, with a blanket over the top to stop the cards slipping too much. But somehow it didn't seem wrong that he didn't play much. Playing wasn't his thing. He was a worker, and that took most of his time and energy.

He worked selling farm machinery for an agricultural supplies company. I can remember as a small boy going into 'the shop' with him, and clambering into the driver's seat of the tractors, and exploring the dark, musty lofts where the seed was stored. I had no idea at the time, of course, how emotionally and physically draining work was for him, and why he used to go to sleep in his chair after dinner. I have some appreciation of it now.

Like many men of my generation, I can't suppress the wish that Dad had played a little more; that he'd been more the kind of intimate, caring dad who gives you hugs, and talks to you about your day. But that wasn't him. It wasn't his style. He was of the generation of men who said, "You'll be wanting to speak to mother" after about 15 seconds of conversation when I phoned home from college.

The question is: What is my style? And is it fixed and unchangeable, or should I try to change my personality so as to be a better dad?

As I talk to other fathers about these sorts of things, they talk about two stereotypes that they find themselves falling into. I'll call them the Captain and the Nice-Guy.

The Captain is Christopher Plummer's character in *The Sound of Music,* or if your knowledge of movies runs more to something in the last 20 years, Robert de Niro's sadistic, intimidatory dad from *Meet the Parents*. He's the strong, reserved authoritarian Master and Commander, who runs a tight ship, whose word is law, and who is feared and respected by his children, as he gazes down upon them from the heights of his throne. When there is bedlam in the Payne household, and my attempts to instil order are being none-too-politely ignored by the rampaging savages, I sometimes think to myself, "They'd never try that with Captain von Trapp!"

The Nice-Guy is James Dean's wimpish father in *Rebel Without a Cause,* or Robin Williams's lovable but ineffectual dad from *Mrs Doubtfire*, who has lots of fun with his kids but imposes almost no boundaries, leaving his wife to be the bad cop and clean up the mess. He's the friendly, nice-guy dad whose attempts at telling his kids what to do are ignored, and who has all the presence, authority and leadership of Mr Bean.

• • •

Are they the only options? Or is it possible to take the best of Captain von Trapp and the best of Robin Williams, and come up with the perfect style for the modern dad? To be tough yet tender, respected yet hugged, obeyed yet loved? Robin Williams just about manages it, but only by dressing up as Mrs Doubtfire. My problem is that I tend to get the worst of each, and end up coolly detached and irresponsible, merciless and disorganized, strident and ineffectual!

Is there a model, an example, we can look to and emulate? For many men, the answer is a despairing 'No'. Their own fathers, if they even knew them, offer no example worth copying. But we sense that there should be. Surely it's possible to find the balance? But do we see it?

Chalk up Big Advantage in Being Christian #247: the perfect model of the fatherliness that we long for is found in the portrait of our Heavenly Father, sketched in bold clear strokes across the pages of the Bible. It's everything we'd like to be, and hope in our best moments we might become.

What sort of father is God in the Bible?

Well, he's got the majesty and authority thing well under control. He's unquestionably in charge. He expects obedience, and there are clear consequences for disobedience. But we also continually see him exercise his great power and authority for the sake of others: providing his creation with good things, remaining faithful to his promises, giving good gifts to his children. He gets angry, but he's slow to anger and maintains his steadfast love to thousands. He rebukes his children because he loves them. He patiently teaches and guides them for their good, and he forgives them time and again for their stupidity and wickedness.

Jesus urges his disciples to be like their Father in heaven in Matthew 5:

"You have heard that it was said, 'You shall love your

neighbor and hate your enemy.' But I say to you, Love your enemies and pray for those who persecute you, so that you may be sons of your Father who is in heaven. For he makes his sun rise on the evil and on the good, and sends rain on the just and on the unjust." (Matt 5:43–45)

Note that he's not urging them to be lordly, distant authority-figures, nor even affable nice-guys. He wants them to love their enemies—like God does. He sends his rain on the just and unjust alike, and causes the sun to shine on both the evil and the good. In other words, he faithfully provides for all his creation, even those creatures of his who spit in his face.

Another extraordinary example of God's fatherliness is in Hosea 11. This chapter likens Israel to a wayward son and God to a mistreated father:

"When Israel was a child, I loved him, and out of Egypt I called my son. The more they were called, the more they went away; they kept sacrificing to the Baals and burning offerings to idols. Yet it was I who taught Ephraim to walk; I took them up by their arms, but they did not know that I healed them. I led them with cords of kindness, with the bands of love, and I became to them as one who eases the yoke on their jaws, and I bent down to them and fed them. (Hos 11:1–4)

God has been a great dad to Israel. He's taught them to walk. He's led them along with cords of kindness, like one of those little harnesses toddlers like me used to have in the 60s. He has healed them, loved them, lifted the yoke from their shoulders, and fed them.

Yet they repaid him by kicking him in the teeth. Like children who respond to their father's voice by running further away, Israel (also referred to as 'Ephraim' in this passage) rebelled against their Father and worshipped other gods. And like a father with a disgrace of a son, God would have been quite within his rights to wipe them completely, to disinherit them, to disown them, to destroy them. But notice what he says next:

> "How can I give you up, O Ephraim? How can I hand you over, O Israel? How can I make you like Admah? How can I treat you like Zeboiim? My heart recoils within me; my compassion grows warm and tender. I will not execute my burning anger; I will not again destroy Ephraim; for I am God and not a man, the Holy One in your midst, and I will not come in wrath." (Hos 11:8-9)

I understand what this passage is saying only too well, for I am a man, and not God! When I am 'executing my burning anger' against the kids, there is a certain point when the pressure-cooker explodes, when steam is hissing out of the ears, and they all of a sudden go very quiet and apologetic. "We're sorry, Daddy." But by then it is too late. It is much too late. By that stage there are very few forces in heaven or hell that can prevent the devastation that is to follow. How typical it is of human fathers to vent their anger and frustration against their children.

God, however, is God and not a man. He is altogether different, which is another way of saying that he is the "Holy One". That's what 'holiness' means. It means 'set apart', 'different', 'in a class of its own'. God is holy, and he shows it in this instance by deciding *not* to come in wrath against Israel. His compassion in this case trumps his anger.

It's a wonderful picture of God's kindness and patience towards his wayward people. It's the perfect combination of severity and compassion, of awe-inspiring authority and oceanic mercy.

We could do no better in our quest for a 'style' than to meditate on the character of God, our heavenly Father, and see how in him justice and mercy meet, and power is mixed with gentleness.

Most of us, according to our personalities, lean towards one end of the spectrum or the other. We're by nature more Leonard Teale than Robin Williams, or vice versa. And so different ones of us will have to work on one aspect or the other. Some of us need to learn how to be tough; others need to learn to express our strength in gentleness.

The Bible offers encouragement in both directions. To the overly strict, God says, "Fathers, do not provoke your children to anger, but bring them up in the discipline and instruction of the Lord" (Eph 6:4). Don't assume, in other words, that being the strict disciplinarian is a virtue in itself.

Beware becoming the father who over-controls his children, who picks them up for every little thing, who never cuts them any slack, who forgets that children are sometimes annoying and frustrating not through evil intent or disobedience, but just because they're kids.

For the overly lenient, God provides the tragic example of Eli, the Old Testament priest of Israel whose delinquent sons were a public disgrace. Instead of serving God at the tabernacle, they basically served themselves, treating the sacrifices with contempt and sleeping with the women who assisted there. Eli goes down and gives them a good talking to, but they take no notice, and Eli does nothing further about it. When God finally judges the two boys, he also judges Eli along with them "because his sons were blaspheming God, and he did not restrain them" (1 Sam 3:13).

This in fact is true strength: to be strong as iron when confronting problems and difficulties, and not to yield in the face of pressure; to follow through on our words and restrain our children when it is needed. And yet also to be strong enough within ourselves to open up and play with our children, and let them be close to us. It's not an overabundance of strength that prevents fathers being gentle, caring and intimate with their children. Often it is the deeply insecure man, the man whose soul is weak and fragile, who cannot open up to a child, be silly with them, praise them openly, and hug them affectionately.

The very attractive thing about the Bible's view of fatherhood is that it avoids the two characteristic errors that have beset human fatherhood throughout history. The 'style' of the biblical father is authority and respect without tyranny and abuse; love and kindness without weakness and neglect. And it owes this marvellous balancing act to the Heavenly Father who created human fatherhood.

PART II
WHAT'S IT ALL FOR?

CHAPTER 7
WHY BOTHER?

So FAR WE'VE tried to answer the question: What is fatherhood? And we came up with a threefold answer:

a. It is giving life to your children.

b. It is lovingly sustaining and nurturing them.

c. It is having authority to do b.

At a time when no-one is too sure what a father is anymore, this is a picture of fatherhood that our society desperately needs. It's a picture that reflects the kind of fatherhood we see in God—the mighty life-giver, the loving ruler, the faithful provider. And one of the beauties of this picture is that it avoids the twin traps that have always bedevilled fathers—of self-centred oppressiveness on the one hand, and sentimental ineffectiveness on the other.

With this picture before our eyes—or etched onto our brains—we have a solid basis for knowing what we're on about, and becoming better dads. And we talked about what that might mean in practice.

However, there was a very important question that we

left hanging. It's the question: *What's it all for?*

We raise our families, we fulfil our responsibilities, we do our best, and our kids turn out okay. But why? For what purpose?

Well, in one sense so that our kids can in turn have their own kids, and raise their families and fulfil their responsibilities so that their kids turn out okay. But is that all? Is human life simply an endless reproductive cycle—we raise kids who raise kids who raise kids ad infinitum—but to no other purpose. Are we just on this merry-go-round that in the end goes nowhere?

The question we left hanging really is: *What's the meaning and purpose of life?* If there is none, then we might as well just have as much fun along the way as we can, be as happy as we can, and try to help our kids be as happy as they can. We might as well eat, drink and be merry, for before too long we'll be dead and it won't count for anything.

We will not have any real purpose as fathers—any goal in mind for ourselves, our kids or our families—because there is no goal. There's just stuff to do and to acquire, and every day above ground is a good day.

But if there *is* a purpose to life, then fatherhood might have a purpose, and raising our kids might have a purpose. There might be a reason for what we do—a goal, a destination, a mission even.

That's what we're going to look at in the second half of

this book. We're going to think about whether fathers have a purpose or destiny, and, if so, what it is.

LET'S GET STARTED with this quick quiz. Mentally put a tick next to any of the following ideas that you find yourself thinking from time to time:

- I think my job is quite significant, and makes a difference in the world.
- I might not be able to give my kids everything, but I can work hard to give them a secure future.
- Humanity has its problems, but we seem to be making progress in solving them; I think the next generation will be better off than ours.
- If only we had just a few thousand more per year, it would make the difference; then we'd be happy.
- I'm not working for myself; I'm working to pass it on to my kids.
- Things were better in the old days; everything's going downhill.
- If you've got your health, well that's the main thing.
- If I can get my kids into good schools, and give them a good education, then they'll have a good career and be happy.
- I really want to do something significant with my life so that I'm remembered when I'm gone.

If you placed any mental ticks, then it may be time for you

take a dip in the icy waters of one of my favourite biblical books, 'The Preacher Man'.

(It's more often called 'Ecclesiastes', but the original Hebrew title in the Old Testament is literally 'The Preacher', which reminds me of the grim 'Preacher Man' characters in classic Westerns, with their dark, worn suits and black hats. Like Clint Eastwood in *Pale Rider*; the kind of Preacher Man who also carried a gun and dispensed bullets along with his sermons.)

Reading 'The Preacher Man' is like waking up from a dream, or having a bucket of cold water thrown on you while you're snoozing on the sofa. Not for him any soft, sentimental sermons about being nice to each other. He casts his searching eye on life as it's lived in the real world, and calls it how he sees it. As he looks around, and as he tries various life-experiments himself, he comes to two basic conclusions:

- Nothing ever really changes.
- One of the things that never changes is that life is unjust and absurd.

Listen to what he says on the meaningless repetitiveness of life, for example:

> What does man gain by all the toil at which he toils under the sun?
> A generation goes, and a generation comes, but the earth remains forever.

The sun rises, and the sun goes down, and hastens to the place where it rises.
The wind blows to the south and goes around to the north; around and around goes the wind, and on its circuits the wind returns.
All streams run to the sea, but the sea is not full; to the place where the streams flow, there they flow again.
All things are full of weariness; a man cannot utter it; the eye is not satisfied with seeing, nor the ear filled with hearing.
What has been is what will be, and what has been done is what will be done,
and there is nothing new under the sun. (Eccl 1:3-9)

Hard to argue with really. We slave our guts out at whatever we're doing, but for what? So that we can keep this creaking bag of flesh and bones going for 70 or 80 years before we drop dead, and some other bag of flesh and bones steps into our place. And how long will it be before we're forgotten by all except our closest relatives? 10 years perhaps? 20 at the most?

And if we console ourselves with the idea that at least we're trying to set our children up and give them a prosperous future, well how do we know that they will even get to enjoy it, given how unjust and uncertain life is? Or that they won't be fools and blow all our hard-earned assets on some dot-com investment?

We make all these plans, says The Preacher Man, but

we can't control the outcome. It's just as likely to end in tears, and then what have we worked for? A vapour. A breath of wind that slips through our fingers and is gone. It's all absurd.

And in case we weren't already fully awake to what kind of world we really live in, he takes a look around and describes it like this:

> Again I saw all the oppressions that are done under the sun. And behold, the tears of the oppressed, and they had no one to comfort them! On the side of their oppressors there was power, and there was no one to comfort them. And I thought the dead who are already dead more fortunate than the living who are still alive. But better than both is he who has not yet been and has not seen the evil deeds that are done under the sun. (Eccl 4:1-3)

And he didn't even have cable television. Life is repetitive, meaningless and, for a vast number of people, fundamentally unjust. The rich rip off the poor, and there's no-one who can do much about it. Maybe we'd just be better off dead, or better yet, unborn, so that our eyes didn't have to look at it.

And in case you weren't already thoroughly depressed, he hits rock bottom with this cheery thought:

> I said in my heart with regard to the children of man

that God is testing them that they may see that they themselves are but beasts. For what happens to the children of man and what happens to the beasts is the same; as one dies, so dies the other. They all have the same breath, and man has no advantage over the beasts, for all is vanity. All go to one place. All are from the dust, and to dust all return. (Eccl 3:18-20)

When it all comes down to it, it seems we're just slightly sophisticated animals, who live, breathe, eat, reproduce and die, so that the next generation can do the same—with the exception that we delude ourselves into thinking that we're other than this; that somehow we are significant and meaningful, and that our lives have purpose.

It's a depressing picture, all the more so because in our hearts we know it's accurate. We drug ourselves into not noticing these sorts of things by keeping busy, and by trying to punctuate our lives with moments of enjoyment—the weekend football, going out with friends, watching TV, and so on.

But it's just bread and circuses. We can distract ourselves and try to numb the pain, but it doesn't change the way things are.

• • •

Now what has all this got to do with fatherhood?

Quite a lot, as it happens. The Preacher Man's wisdom is a powerful antidote to the mental viruses that fathers commonly suffer from. And these viruses are all false answers to the question that we're looking at in this part of the book: *What is a father for? What's his purpose or goal?* We get infected with false or misleading answers to these questions from various sources, and this diseased thinking lodges in our brains and does damage. These mental viruses are things like this:

- What I really want to achieve as a father is to help my kids have a prosperous and happy life.
- My goal as a dad is to give my kids all those things I missed out on when I was growing up.
- I might not have fulfilled my own dreams, but I want to give my kids the chance to fulfil theirs.
- If I can raise my kids just to be happy, well-adjusted people, making their own contribution to society, I'll have succeeded as a dad.
- My goal in life is to build up a nest egg to pass on to my kids—if I can set them up for life by the time I die, I'll have succeeded.
- If I can give my kids the opportunity to succeed—to have a fulfilling career with good money—then I'll have achieved my goals as a dad.

A little dose of The Preacher Man tells us that these

answers are misleadingly half-true or stupidly blind to the realities of life. It's a tragic, foolish waste of time, says the Preacher, to labour and toil so as to accumulate wealth to pass on to kids, because only one of two things will follow: either they will squander it, and you'll have worked for nothing; or they'll make good use of it in order to accumulate enough wealth to pass on to their kids who will then either squander it or pass it on to their kids—and on it goes, round and round, meaninglessly repeating itself, to no purpose whatsoever. That's the kind of labour that a hamster toils at as he treads his endlessly-turning little wheel, which passes beneath his feet then up and over his head, and then back round beneath his feet again.

Very well, you may say, I won't worry too much about the inheritance—I'll just try to give my kids a good and happy life by giving them lots of opportunities. But what, in the end, is the use of that? For one thing, wealth and prosperity are fleeting; they're here one minute and often gone the next. All your years of toil and investment and heartache can soon melt away. And even if you do manage to be prosperous and give your kids every opportunity in the world, what guarantee of happiness is it for either you or them? Why are rich kids, with all the opportunities in the world, just as miserable and prone to drug abuse (and they can afford it) as working-class kids?

The message of The Preacher Man, which he rams

home with relentless clarity, is that every attempt to define our own meaning and purpose in life—by our work, our possessions, our cleverness, our pleasures, our families, anything—is doomed to fail. Life is too unpredictable, unjust and absurd to allow us to succeed. And death makes fools and beasts of us all.

In fact, he puts it even more starkly. He says that *God* has made it this way so that we won't get ahead of ourselves. It's the burden God has laid on humanity: to understand and know enough about the world to know that some things are good and worth having (like satisfaction in our work and food on our table), and some things aren't (like oppression, poverty and death). But we can't find the meaning or the purpose of it all. We can't comprehend the whole thing. We don't know where the world is heading, or where *we're* heading. Whenever we take a step back and try to make sense of it, it's a confused and confusing jumble of contradictions.

We need to beat this into our brains because our culture tells us just the opposite all the time. It whispers in our ear: "Your goal as a father should be to keep climbing, keep improving your position, keep moving up a suburb when you can, buy the next model up, it's all for your kids, they deserve the best, make sure they get into good schools, steer them towards promising careers, give them every opportunity, so that they can get into uni, because they need to develop their potential, so that they can have a bright and promising future ...". And on it goes, the unspoken creed that we all know by heart.

Hang on, you may say, I thought I was supposed to be a faithful and loving sustainer and nurturer of my family. I thought I was supposed to generously provide good things for them.

Quite right. We created them—we should take care of them, teaching and feeding and nurturing them to maturity. *But what for? To what end?* What do we want them to achieve in their maturity, when they have fulfilled all that potential we have so lovingly fostered? What's the overriding purpose of it all?

If there is none, we might as well be as rich as we can, live in the best house in the best suburb we can afford, and have as much pleasure as we can in the short time we have on earth.

If there *is* a purpose, but we can't figure it out, we could do a lot worse than follow the Preacher's advice—just fear God and obey his commandments, because he will sort everything out in the end.

But if there is a purpose to life, and we can know what it is—if it all means something and is headed somewhere —then that changes everything. Your own life as a father, and the lives of your kids, would have a direction, a purpose, an intent. There would be something to shoot for, a goal to aim at, a destination that would determine your journey.

Is there somewhere to find this meaning or purpose? The Preacher Man didn't seem to think so.

But there was something that he didn't know.

CHAPTER 8
THE DAY EVERYTHING CHANGED

I'VE NEVER BEEN a huge fan of movies with subtitles, for reasons that I can't really explain. Perhaps it just seems like more of an effort than watching movies should be. Or maybe it was some bad experiences I had as a student, where we all went off to art-house cinemas to show how sophisticated we were by watching four hours of *Celine and Julie go boating*, or some other supposed masterpiece of French cinema.

In any case, I recently stepped outside my comfort zone and saw a German movie called *Good Bye Lenin!* It's set in the communist East German side of Berlin in 1989, just before the Wall came down and the East German government collapses. It centres around a woman named Christiane and her son Alex. Christiane is a pillar of the communist society. She passionately believes in the benefits of socialism, and works tirelessly for the workers, writing reports and petitions, organizing social programs, going to party meetings, and so on. She is admired and given numerous awards by the communist authorities for her heroic work for the benefit of the workers.

But then Christiane has an accident and falls into a coma. While she is unconscious, the momentous events of 1989 unfold, and her world changes. By the time she wakes up from the coma, the communist government has collapsed, capitalism is breaking out all over East Berlin, and the process that would eventually lead to the reunification of Germany has already begun. But of course, in one of those narrative twists so beloved of movie directors, Christiane's health is still delicate, and her son Alex is told that she should be spared any shocks or anxieties of any kind. Alex realizes that if his mother were to find out that her beloved socialist state has collapsed, and that everything she believed in and worked so tirelessly for has been overturned, the shock would be fatal. And so he decides to try to keep his mother in the dark about what has happened, by recreating the old East Germany in the little house in which they live. He enlists the support of his sister, and his mother's friends and colleagues and neighbours; they secretly feed old East German videos into the TV so that she thinks she's watching what's happening now; and so on. The results are hilarious, and quite touching.

Christiane lives on as if nothing has changed, even though it is in defiance of reality. Despite the success of Alex's schemes to shield her from the truth, the brute facts were inescapable—the world *had* changed, almost overnight. The Wall was down. The communist state had collapsed. Nothing would ever be the same.

Christians sometimes live in a *Good Bye Lenin!* world. Our familiarity with the core elements of our faith—the death of Jesus for our sins, his resurrection, his Lordship over all—can sometimes blind us to their significance. We can blunder along on our way through life almost as if these things hadn't happened, or as if they make no difference to the way the world is; as if the world is still the way it was before the momentous events of Christ.

But the events that took place around 33 AD concerning Jesus of Nazareth were like the breaking down of the Berlin Wall and the collapse of East German communism. They were momentous history-making events that completely altered the landscape and changed the world forever. And if we are aware that they have in fact happened—that is, if we're not in a coma or living in an artificial dream world—then they must change everything about our lives.

What was it that happened?

You know the events themselves. I don't have to describe them in any detail. A Jewish man with a massive popular following was executed by the authorities on trumped up charges, and then on the third day following his death, came back triumphant from the dead with a body that was visible and 'physical', and yet different in some way from normal human flesh and blood. After being seen in this way by many of his followers, he left this earth to ascend to the spiritual realm of his God and Father.

If the accounts in the Gospels are true, this is what happened. I won't bother mounting the argument at this point as to why the Gospels are very likely to be accurate on these points—others have covered this ground in detail (see the *Further Reading* at the end of the book).

What I want to clarify before we go any further is *just what was happening* when these events took place. When East Germany collapsed, certain events took place. A gate was opened to allow people from one side to pass through to another. Some barricades in front of a wall were removed, and certain people knocked a hole in the wall. The head of a political party resigned. These are the bare events. What they signified was that a whole political order was being swept away. A state of affairs that had existed for more than 40 years was being overturned, seemingly overnight. That's what was really going on.

What was really going on when this man Jesus was so cruelly killed, and then rose from the dead?

The apostle Peter explains it pretty simply in his first major speech after all these things happened. He stands in front of a large crowd of fellow Jews and says:

> Let all the house of Israel therefore know for certain that
> God has made him both Lord and Christ, this Jesus
> whom you crucified. (Acts 2:36)

What was happening in the extraordinary events of 33 AD was that a man—a flesh and blood human, who was able to be killed like any other man—had been appointed to a unique position. God had made him "Lord and Christ". 'Lord' is a word we know, meaning master or ruler. 'Christ' means 'anointed one', which was the Jewish way (at that time) of saying 'God's Chosen King of All the World'.[4]

So Peter was saying that this man Jesus, who had been executed less than two months previously, had risen from the dead, had ascended to God's right hand on high, and had been appointed by God as ruler and king of all the world.

If Peter was right about this, then the world was a different place than it was two months previously. It had a new ruler, a new Lord: the man Jesus was now the Christ, the Lord of everything. (As it turned out, he was also God's own Son, who had come to earth in human flesh, but that's another part of the story.)

Now, says Peter, this is the current state of affairs. This is how things are. Jesus is the Christ of all the world. So what are you going to do about it?

For Peter's original hearers and for us there are only two possible responses to a change in government of this nature: you go with it, and submit to the new government; or you reject it, either by actively resisting, or by simply ignoring its authority and continuing to live as if nothing has changed.

Someone who submits to the government of Jesus the Christ, and obeys him as the ruler of all things, is called a 'Christian'. Many people, of course, want nothing to do with this Christ. Some are active rebels, quite deliberately rejecting what they regard as the illegitimate 'lordship' of this Jesus; others are passive rebels, who just get on with life and ignore the whole thing, with an unstated but deep belief that Jesus is either not really the Lord, or else won't mind if they stay out of his way.

If you're reading this book, and you're not a Christian—that is, you have not submitted to the supreme lordship of Jesus Christ in this world—then I'd recommend that you rethink your position with some urgency. You need to be very sure in your own mind that Jesus is *not* the Lord of all—that he did not rise from the dead to God's right hand, and that the New Testament's record of these things is false or unreliable. It's not the kind of life-choice to make without reasonable evidence and a bit of thought, because you're deciding to be a rebel against the supreme governor of the world—if this is in fact his position. If you get it wrong, you're in serious trouble, as the rest of the New Testament makes fairly plain. A day is coming when he will return to this earth in his position as its Lord and King and crush all those who oppose him, consigning them to an eternal destruction that doesn't bear thinking about. You'd want to be fairly sure in your own mind that you knew what you were doing before you took up this position.

If the claims of the New Testament are true, and there has been a change of government in our world, with Jesus Christ having been appointed the Supreme President, then to keep living as if this is not the case is like being Christiane in *Good Bye Lenin!* You can keep up the charade for a while, but it breaks down eventually. Reality has a way of sneaking up on you and hitting you over the head with a length of four-by-two.

Sadly, Christians can end up living in the *Good Bye Lenin!* dream world as well. They allow themselves to be lulled to sleep. Their lips continue to form the words 'Jesus is Lord', but in their hearts it has no power, and in their lives it shows no impact. Their lives meander on almost indistinguishable from the non-Christians around them, as if the world had not changed on that day nearly 2000 years ago when Jesus Christ rose in glory—as if there were no Lord of the World, no Christ, no Ruler and Judge who is coming again.

This is tragic, not to mention faithless, short-sighted and stupid, and I suppose I could spend some paragraphs berating Christians on this point.

However, I want to move on to a more important point, which picks up where we left off at the end of the last chapter. The death and resurrection of Jesus Christ and his subsequent appointment as world ruler, is something that the Preacher of Ecclesiastes didn't know about or expect. And although it doesn't solve all the puzzles of existence, or the fundamentally confusing and absurd nature of daily life, it does reveal the answer to the very important question we've been considering: *What's it all for?* (which includes the meaning of life in general, and of being a father in particular).

On the day that everything changed—the day Jesus ascended to be the Christ and Lord of all—God revealed the answer to the question. He made public where the world is going, where our lives are going, and what his plans are for each one of us. This is because the Lordship of Christ is the climax of a history-long plan by God to fix up the mess we've made of the world, to bring reconciliation with God where there once was hostility, to create unity where there was division, to breathe new life into the dead, to set everything to rights again. In Ephesians, the apostle Paul puts it like this:

[In Christ, he made known] to us the mystery of his will, according to his purpose, which he set forth in Christ as a plan for the fullness of time, to unite all things in him, things in heaven and things on earth. (Eph 1:9-10)

What Paul is basically saying is that God has always had a plan running—that there has always been a purpose and direction to human history, and for human lives. It's just that for quite a while the climax of that plan was a secret. With the coming of Christ, the secret has been revealed. We now know what the end point of the plan is: it's for everything in heaven and on earth to be united or gathered together in Christ. It's for him to be Lord of everything, to fix everything, to complete everything. Instead of us being sinners and enemies of God, we may be forgiven and reconciled to him. Instead of being divided from each other and hating each other, we can be united together as fellow subjects and servants of Jesus Christ, who love him and each other.

That's the purpose and meaning of life, and of each one of our lives individually. It's what we've been created for. We aren't meaningless lumps of molecules; nor are we independent beings who give our own lives meaning and significance. We are creatures. We've been made by Someone Else, and that Someone Else determines the purpose of his creation (as all creators do). The lie that we so easily accept is that we are *not* creatures; that we are 'self-made men' who decide for ourselves what our lives will be about.

The purpose for which God made us—the destiny towards which all of us are heading—is to submit to Jesus Christ, and to be reconciled through him with God our

Father. Christ is the one who gives meaning to history, to our individual lives, and to the lives of our kids. Your destiny, and your family's destiny, is to be found in him, in the man who died and rose and is now the ruler of all things.

Now you can pretend that this is not the case. You can go on living as if Jesus Christ is not the Lord of all who determines the purpose of your life. You can go on raising your kids, and mowing the lawn, and paying the bills, and watching TV as if there is not a Christ whose subject you are, whose world you live in. But that would be to retreat into a make-believe world; to pretend that things are other than they really are; that there has not been a change of government.

The fact of the Lordship of Jesus Christ, and God's purpose to unite all things under him, means that our lives have a purpose. Our lives have a direction, a goal, a destiny, which affects everything, including fatherhood.

In the next two chapters, I want to explore what this means for being a father. What is the purpose for which God has made us fathers? What's it all *for*?

ENDNOTE

4. The background to this is that Israelite kings were 'anointed' with oil at their coronations. The 'anointed one' was the king chosen by God to rule. And by this time in Jewish history, they were looking forward to One who had been promised for hundreds of years, who would be the Anointed One (capital A, capital O), who would be king not just of Israel but of the whole world.

CHAPTER 9

THE DISCIPLE

PICTURE THE SCENE. A lonely and deserted place, somewhere in the region of Caesarea Philippi in Galilee, in northern Palestine. A dusty road stretches south into the distance towards Samaria, and then eventually to Jerusalem. To one side of the road, a group of men are seated talking. And another man is a little further away on his own, praying.

The man—who is Jesus—walks over to his followers. They have recently been out and about among the villages and towns, spreading their Master's message. Jesus asks them for a status report: "What are people saying about me? Who do the crowds think I am?"

Various answers come back, all along the lines that he is one of the great ones of the past come back to life—John the Baptist, Elijah or a prophet. Jesus then makes the question more personal: "What about you? Who do you think I am?"

Peter, who is usually the first one to open his mouth in these circumstances, most often to insert his foot in it, speaks up. And for once he gets it right first time. "The

Christ of God", he says.

It's an extraordinary thing to say. There they are, in the back-blocks of Galilee, a long way from Jerusalem and the centre of the nation's life. Just twelve very ordinary men and their teacher, talking alone. And Peter says to his teacher, "You are the King that God has chosen to rule Israel and the whole world" (remember, that's what 'Christ' means).

It's hard to imagine how far away ruling the world must have seemed to Peter and his friends. But something about Jesus had made them believe that he was indeed the One; that he would rise to power, smash the stranglehold of the Roman occupiers, and lead Israel to a glorious, new, world-dominating golden age. In one sense, looking at this bunch of men chatting with their Master, it seems about as likely as saying that Jesus was John the Baptist or Elijah come back to life.

What Jesus says next, however, is even more startling and shocking, especially to his followers. He doesn't contradict Peter, but he tells him to keep his opinion quiet. And then he tells him why. Jesus points down the road towards Jerusalem, and says, "Now is not the time for glory and for rule. It is not the time for Christs to be sitting on thrones. Something else has to happen first. I have to walk down that road to Jerusalem. And when I get there, the elders and chief priests and scribes will reject me and spit on me and beat me. And kill me. And after that, only after that, I will rise."

By this time, a crowd has started to gather. And Jesus turns to them and says (if I can continue to paraphrase), "That's where I'm going. Down that road to Jerusalem, and when I get there I'm going to be mistreated and cruci-fied. If you want to follow me, be my guest. But it's a long road, and at the end of it is suffering and death. If you want to come with me, you'll have to get up each morning and throw the cross up on your shoulder, and get ready to lose your life. Of course, by losing it you'll also save it, because after the suffering and death will come the victory that I'm going to win. And that victory will mean your salvation. But you've got to realize that before the glory comes the suffering and death.

"So be careful what you choose to do. Come with me, if you're ready to deny any claim on your own life. And if you do that, you'll live and be saved. But if you stay here and play it safe, well you'll avoid the suffering that lies down that road. The only thing is, you'll eventually lose everything when I come into my glory. If you won't walk with me now, I won't recognize you then, when I claim my kingdom." (See Luke 9:18-27.)

For us, 20 centuries later, the idea of 'following Jesus' is a nice, abstract sort of religious idea. We associate it with being moral like Jesus was, imitating him, following his teaching, and generally going with the vibe of Jesus in any given situation. But I sometimes wonder what it would have been like, being in the crowd on that day near Caesarea Philippi, hearing that challenge from Jesus' own lips. There was nothing abstract or sentimental about it. "I'm going that-a-way", he said, pointing down the road to Jerusalem. "I'm going to walk into the jaws of suffering and death. Who wants to come and die with me?"

I can imagine standing there, looking down the road towards Jerusalem, and thinking, "I bet he's right, too. They'll never accept him. If he goes there, he'll end up dead. And he wants me to go with him, and to die at his side."

I can imagine thinking about my wife and kids at home. What will happen to them if I head off on this wild goose-chase with this so-called Christ? Who'll pay the rent? Who'll plough the fields? What if he's wrong, and there's no salvation at the end of the rainbow?

I can imagine weighing up the odds. One side: I go with him, probably die, and hope that his promise about this being the only way to 'save my life' is true. The other side: stay here, play the percentages, and bank on the fact that there is no way that this backwoods carpenter guy from Nazareth with the long hair and the sandals is ever going to be the glorious king of the world.

Of course, from where we now stand, 20 centuries later, this side of the cross and the resurrection, the odds look a bit different. We now know that he *was* rejected, beaten and killed, and on the third day *did* rise again, to be appointed by God as the Ruler of the World, the majestic Christ. We know that on the other side of the suffering there *was* glory. And we know that the choice we are faced with is whether to submit to this Christ, who now rules as God, or to continue to ignore and/or reject him.

But although the choice may seem clearer and even more stark to us now, standing where we do, it's not really any different from the choice that faced the crowd, standing by the road, twenty centuries ago. To choose to follow this Christ is to choose the path of suffering, hardship, self-denial and death in this world. It means committing ourselves to him totally, obeying him, learning from him, following his example. In the words of Jesus, it means *losing your life*.

This is the level of commitment that Jesus asks for, if we are going to be his followers. He calls on us to say 'No' to ourselves, to deny ourselves, and to follow him.

We don't like this. I certainly don't. It feels crushing and humiliating. Why must we say 'No' to ourselves? Why must we 'deny' ourselves? What's wrong with my life that I'm forced to give it up, to lose it, to place it entirely at his disposal? Jesus has his own life: why does he want mine as well? Is it a power thing—that he will only be happy when everyone is utterly subservient to his will?

All humans have an instantaneous sense of resistance to the call of Jesus to deny ourselves and follow him. It's because all of us, without exception, are in love with the idea that we are not really creatures. We relish the thought that we are the captains of our own souls, and that our lives are ours to do with as we determine. We call this 'human freedom', but it is the freedom of the madman who lives in a fantasy world.

The reality is that we *are* creatures, that we have been created by a good and generous God, and that our lives have a meaning and purpose determined by him. He has made us for fellowship and friendship with himself. Our purpose or destiny is in him through his Son, Jesus Christ.

In saying 'No' to ourselves, we are not saying no to something true. We are saying 'No' to the lie that we are our own little gods, who determine the reality of our own little worlds. In saying 'Yes' to Christ, we are set free to pursue the true meaning and destiny of our lives, for which we were created—a destiny that Jesus summarizes simply as 'his glory'. In denying ourselves, we are saying 'No' to the false, rebellious fantasy that God is not God.

John Calvin, the Reformer of the 16th century, called this 'self-denial' the 'sum of the Christian life'. We are not our own, but God's:

We are not our own: let us not, therefore, use our own reason or will to determine our plans or deeds. We are not our own: let us not, therefore, make it our goal to seek what is expedient for ourselves. We are not our own: in so far as we can, let us therefore forget ourselves and all that is ours.

Conversely, we are God's: let us therefore live for him and die for him. We are God's: let his wisdom and will therefore rule all our actions. We are God's: let all the parts of our life strive toward him as our only rightful goal …

Let this therefore be the first step: that a man depart from himself in order that he may apply the whole force of his ability in the service of the Lord.[5]

Here is the purpose, goal and destiny of our lives as humans, as men, as fathers. It is to be a disciple of Jesus: to live for him and die for him, "to let all the parts of our life strive toward him as our only rightful goal". This is what gives meaning to the chaos and absurdity and unpredictability and boredom and hardship and suffering of life, as well as to its pleasures and joys. It all has a purpose and a goal, because it's all part of our daily self-denying, cross-bearing journey of discipleship.

First and above all else, our goal as Christian fathers is to follow Jesus, to walk in his footsteps down the hard, narrow, straight road of discipleship. This is the One Thing that drives us, and which takes priority over all else.

Even over family.

Jesus himself makes that clear enough to his disciples

not long after they had started their long journey to Jerusalem. As he is walking along the road, he calls on someone to follow him, and the man says, "Lord, let me first go and bury my father". To which Jesus replies, "Your father has died? Look, that's terrible. I'm so sorry. Would you like me to spend some time with your family? You never know, I might even be able to do something about your father."

Well, not exactly. His reply (as Luke records it for us in Luke 9:60) is stark and uncompromising: "Leave the dead to bury their own dead. But as for you, go and proclaim the kingdom of God". Even the very strong social obligations of burying a family member—even one's own father—don't override the call of the kingdom.

In the next verse, someone has an excuse that seems equally reasonable: "I will follow you, Lord, but let me first say farewell to those at my home."

Sounds fair enough—after all, if you're about to go on a suicide mission to Jerusalem, the least you owe the wife and kids is a final tearful hug and goodbye. But again, Jesus is uncompromising. You can't look back, he says. And you can't put anything else 'first'. For that is the recurring word in these verses: let me *first* do this; let me *first* do that. If you are going to follow Jesus down this road, there can be no 'let me first'. Jesus demands immediate, urgent and total commitment, even over our closest human ties.

This idea is not a new one in Luke's Gospel, nor will it be the last time it's mentioned. Earlier, in chapter 8, Jesus' mother and brothers come to see him, but can't even get close because of the crowd. Some helpful soul lets Jesus know that the relatives have arrived and would like to see him, but Jesus responds: "My mother and my brothers are those who hear the word of God and do it" (8:21). Hardly a family-friendly thing to say.

And it happens again in chapter 11. Someone calls out from the crowd, "Blessed is the womb that bore you, and the breasts at which you nursed!" To which you'd think Jesus would say something like, "Yes, she's lovely isn't she, my Mum? I thank God for her every day." But he doesn't take the opportunity to pay Mary a compliment. Instead, he says: "Blessed rather are those who hear the word of God and keep it!" (11:28).

What Jesus is saying in both of these instances is that family ties don't make you special, or get you into the kingdom. It's not having the right surname that makes you a true brother of Jesus, or being related to him that makes you truly blessed. It's how you respond to his words, which are the words of God. It's whether you follow him and obey him; it's whether you hear the word of God and do it.

Easily the starkest and most shocking saying of Jesus about families comes just a couple of chapters later in Luke

14. Massive crowds were following him—which you'd think Jesus would be all in favour of—but he turns to them and says something that almost seems calculated to drive them away. He says, "If anyone comes to me and does not hate his own father and mother and wife and children and brothers and sisters, yes, and even his own life, he cannot be my disciple. Whoever does not bear his own cross and come after me cannot be my disciple" (14:26-27).

Jesus repeats the challenge he issued at the very beginning. If you follow me, you do so at the cost of your very life and everything you hold dear. Carrying your cross means that even your own family come off second best.

'Second best' we might just cope with, but 'hate'? Do we have to loathe and detest our families (a task which some of us will find easier than others)?

The problem is with the word 'hate'. The Greek word that's translated 'hate' in this verse, and in numerous others in Luke's Gospel, has a broader range of meaning than our English word 'hate'. When we say that we 'hate' something, we're saying that we have a very strong aversion to it; we can't stand it; it fills us with emotions of loathing and even disgust. The Greek word can mean this, but it can also mean the simple act of choosing between two options, so that one option is disadvantaged. If you have only one spot left on the football team, and you have to choose between two hopefuls, then you'll end up 'hating' one of them. That is, one of them will miss out, will be rejected by you, and will suffer loss. You might not have anything personal against them, but simply by not choosing them, you've 'hated' them; you've caused them harm and loss.

This is what it means when God says, "Jacob I loved, but Esau I hated".[6] It doesn't mean that God 'hated Esau's guts', that he couldn't stand the sight (or smell) of Esau, and so chose to love Jacob instead. After all, God made his choice before the two were born, before they had done anything to distinguish themselves at all—that's the whole point that Paul is making in Romans 9. To 'hate' in this sense, is simply to disadvantage or disregard or exclude something because you've chosen something else instead. It is in this sense that Jacob loved Rachel and hated Leah (Gen 29:30-31).

To choose Jesus, to deny yourself and follow him with exclusive loyalty, means that by necessity you have excluded all other loyalties. Even your closest kin will suffer because of your choice. They no longer have first call on you. The responsibility you have for them as a father has not changed—the responsibility that comes from having given them life—but that responsibility is not all-encompassing or to the exclusion of all else. It's not your highest and first responsibility.

A moving illustration of this is found in John Bunyan's

famous allegory of the Christian life, *The Pilgrim's Progress*. The story opens with the main character, whose name is 'Christian', in a state of great distress. He has read in a book that the city in which he lives is going to be destroyed, and, believing this report to be true, he decides to flee. When he tells his wife and four sons about it, they are also very concerned—not because they believe him for a minute, but because they think he's gone mad. They put him to bed in the hope that it might settle him down, but the next day, the feeling is only stronger. Christian urges his family to believe him, and to escape with him, but they become increasingly abusive. In the end, he begins to run away alone from the doomed city:

> Now, he had not run far from his own door, but his wife and children, perceiving it, began to cry after him to return; but the man put his fingers in his ears, and ran on, crying, Life! life! eternal life! So he looked not behind him, but fled towards the middle of the plain.

Bunyan manages to portray in this brief picture both the power of family ties, and the need sometimes to ignore them. Christian knows that if he listens to his family's desperate calls for him to come back, if he even hears their voices—the voices of his wife and his sons—that he will not be able to bear it. Yet he knows he must flee, even if they refuse to follow him. The only way he can possibly leave them behind is to put his fingers in his ears and shout "Life! life! eternal life!" so that he cannot hear their cries, and not look back so that he cannot see their desperate faces.

A Christian man is a pilgrim first, and a husband and father second. His first duty is as a disciple. His chief goal is to reach the end of the journey he has embarked upon, which is to follow Christ through suffering and death to glory. With the strength that God the Holy Spirit provides, he will bravely endure the hardship that this journey will bring. And he will not turn back from the journey, or from the obedience and faithfulness that the journey requires, even if the people he loves best in all the world ask him to do so.

In the end, Christianity is not a 'family first' party. We love our families, we affirm their importance, we fight for their protection in a society that increasingly seems to devalue and attack them, but they are not our first priority or ultimate value. 'Family' is not a master that rules our lives.

All this is very disturbing, and so it ought to be for a family man. You may be thinking: Why does God put us in a position where we have to choose between him and our families? Aren't we supposed to love and care for our families, and take responsibility for them? Why must we deny them or make them suffer?

The answer to these quite legitimate concerns is simple: we must say 'No' to our families for the same reason we must say 'No' to ourselves. As with our own lives, the destiny of our children doesn't lie in themselves, and in their own purposes, goals and aspirations. It lies in God. That's the purpose of their lives, and where they will find ultimate goodness and freedom. The family does not establish its own purpose and destiny, any more than we do as individuals. The family is not the purpose of life, or the ultimate good. To make it so is to embrace just another form of the lie that humans have always found so attractive—that *we* determine what's important and good and ultimately true, not God.

We cannot worship our families, for that would not only be foolish and idolatrous, but also ultimately destructive of the very ones we love. We must show them by our own example that all human lives find their fulfilment and purpose in only one place: in Christ. Choosing to deny ourselves and follow him will mean suffering in this world, but it is ultimately the path of freedom and glory.

• • •

FAIR ENOUGH, you may say, but what does that mean in practice? Am I saying that when our kids ask us to kick a ball in the backyard, good Christian fathers should put our fingers in our ears and shout "Life! life! eternal life!" and return to our reading of the seven seals of Revelation? Given we have a responsibility to our families, not to mention the demands of our work as well, how is the priority of discipleship worked out in practice?

Here are five suggestions.

1. Don't listen

The modern man is supposed to be a good listener, and no doubt many of us could lift our game in this area. When our wives want to pour out the troubles and frustrations of their day, something more than the occasional grunt from behind the newspaper is usually helpful. But there's an important biblical sense in which we must *not* listen to our wives and children, if we are to be good disciples of Jesus Christ.

When the very first man sinned, God made clear to Adam what his problem was: "Because you have listened to the voice of your wife and have eaten of the tree of which I commanded you, 'You shall not eat of it,' cursed is the ground because of you …" (Gen 3:17).

Interestingly, a few chapters later in Genesis, Abram makes the same mistake. He's been promised a great multitude of descendants by God, but has a slight problem. His wife Sarai is barren, and there seems no prospect that this is going to change. Sarai comes up with a plan. Perhaps if God is preventing her from having children, the promise could still be fulfilled by Abram having children by the servant girl, Hagar. Abram should have realized that: a) taking matters into their own hands like this was not the way to gain God's blessing; b) Hagar was an Egyptian, and this was hardly the method by which God would create a whole new nation for himself; and c) that even if they succeeded in getting a son through Hagar, it would only lead to problems between Sarai and Hagar (which it did).

Sarai's plan was dodgy in the extreme. But in Genesis 16:2, it says that when she told him about it, "Abram listened to the voice of Sarai", and went along with it. In other words, it was Adam and Eve all over again.

There is a time for listening, and a time for taking no notice. When our wives or children propose something that is not the way for a disciple of Jesus Christ to live, we must not follow their advice. When our kids are urging us to spend up big on a plasma television when we know that the money would be better spent on some other more important need, then we shouldn't listen to them just to keep them happy. Or when they want to see certain movies that we judge aren't at all appropriate for their age, we should put our fingers in our ears (metaphorically speaking) when they protest. Or when our wife can't or won't to go to church, that shouldn't stop us from going. And so on.

Being a disciple means listening to our Lord and Master first, and not accepting any advice or urgings that contradict his word to us—even if it is from the beloved wife and children.

2. Divide the time

Being a disciple first will work itself out in a multitude of daily decisions. It's a mindset or framework that will influence everything we do—including how we allocate time to different areas of our lives.

This is a huge issue for many fathers. If there's one topic of conversation that comes up repeatedly over coffee at church, or after touch rugby on the walk home, it's 'the juggling act'. There are just so many balls in the air. Everywhere you turn, there's someone else who wants a piece of your time: your boss, your wife, your kids, your church, your friends (if you have any left). How do you keep them all happy? Or given that it's impossible, how do you stop too many of the balls going splat at the same time?

From my conversations, the big five for Christian fathers are: work, wife, kids, rest and church. They are all important and necessary, and they all need at least some time devoted to them. Any one of them can be over-emphasized to the detriment of the others. It seems to me that the three most common imbalances are:

- investing too much time in **work**, either because we love the satisfaction, significance and recognition it gives us, or because we're so committed to the lifestyle that our income makes possible that we're not prepared to compromise;
- being so wrapped up in our **kids**, and their activities and education, that everything else comes off second best, including our marriages and our involvement in church; and
- trying to maintain a range of **leisure** activities that were quite sustainable when we were in our mid-twenties, but now chew up too high a proportion of our time (as a passionate golfer, this one is close to home).

Perhaps most common of all is the combination effect that leaves one or other of the big five completely neglected— for example, keeping the balls labelled 'work', 'wife', 'kids' and 'leisure' in the air, but allowing the one labeled 'church' to hit the ground and roll quietly into the corner. Or being so busy working hard, running around after the kids, and being involved in church, that you and your wife hardly know each other any more.

We each have our own problems, and I can no more

dictate precise solutions in this area than I could tell you which mobile phone package would suit you best. The important thing is that as a disciple of Jesus, you prayerfully and thoughtfully consider how your time is being spent. Where are the gaps and the imbalances? To adapt an old chestnut, if you were asked to keep timesheets for three months, and then on that basis to stand trial before God, would there be enough evidence to convict you as a disciple of Christ? Does your commitment to Christ *drive* the way you allocate your time?

Some of our time allocations are 'fixed' (such as being at work for a certain number of hours, or needing to eat and sleep); others are 'variable' (such as choosing to work overtime, what we do in the evenings when we get home, and so on). Here's an exercise that you might find useful: try keeping a record for two weeks of how all your *variable* time is spent, in half-hour units, under these categories:

- overtime
- kids (time spent primarily for their benefit, either in play or in helping with homework)
- wife (time alone with her)
- chores (fixing things, maintenance, shopping, etc.)
- leisure (TV, sport, exercise, time with friends)
- Christian activities (personal or family Bible reading, church, small group, prayer)

Keep a record in your diary or PDA. And then analyse the results. How much total 'variable' time each week did you have? And what percentage, on average, was allocated to the different areas? Do those percentages reflect the priorities you would like to have?

This sort of exercise can be very revealing about where our time is actually going, and what the imbalances are. The next step, of course, is bringing the reality more into line with the ideal.

3. The daily walk

Time allocation is an important subject, but we need to be careful as we deal with it. We must beware of making a false split between the 'Christian' parts of our week, and the 'Christianity-free zone' that is the rest of the week. Although we do need to be deliberate in finding time for personal Bible reading, prayer, church, and so on, it's not as if we cease being Christians when we are not doing these activities.

As disciples, we carry the cross *daily*. It's always on our back, and should dictate how we handle ourselves at work, how we talk to our children at dinner, and how we treat our wives. Each new day is a day to deny ourselves, to say 'No' to our former selfish, rebellious way of life, and to walk in loving obedience to our Saviour.

Here's another inventory worth compiling, since we're in the mood. Have a look through the fruit of the Spirit in

Galatians 5, the characteristics of love in 1 Corinthians 13, and the details of the new lifestyle we are to live as disciples in Colossians 3:1-17. Pray before you read the passages, and ask God to help you see any specific attitudes or behaviours in your life that need to change if you are going to be a faithful disciple. As you read, jot down anything that comes to mind, and then focus in on just two items. Make it your goal over the next three months to work hard on these two problem areas: by prayer, by diligent effort, and by the help and encouragement of others (tell your wife and/or some good friends what you're working on, and get them to pray for you and ask you about it).

There's no harm sharing this exercise with your whole family. As we'll point out in our next chapter, part of taking our children with us on the road of discipleship is letting them see us struggle and strive to make progress in godliness—to see our passion for pursuing holiness. It allows them to see what's really important to us.

4. Convert the wallet

How we spend our money will also indicate what's important to us, where our priorities lie, and what our goals are. It will show whether or not we have grasped what it means to have 'Disciple of Jesus Christ' tattooed on our foreheads.

Fathers, along with their wives, have many decisions to make about family finances—from whether and where to go on holidays, to how much to spend on housing, to whether to keep up your long-term membership of the golf club when you're finding it difficult to get out once a month let alone once a week, and your short-game has disappeared, and you're in danger of losing your golf handicap, and the closest you get to the course is driving past it on Saturday mornings on your way to your daughter's netball match and looking with bitter longing through the fence at the laughing foursome on the 10th green who are probably neglecting their wives and children in order to be there (not that this is a subject close to my heart).

As I reflect on my own experience as a family man trying to make ends meet, I think that I'm more open to compromise, rationalization and ungodliness with regard to money than with almost anything else. The particular form of self-deception I'm most prone to goes like this: "I'm not interested in having a nice home in a nice suburb with a second storey renovation for its *own* sake, or even for *my* sake. I'm doing it for the family. And that's a Christian attitude, because as a Christian I regard my family as a top priority. What greater responsibility does a Christian father have than to provide for his kids? And I'm going to make sure I fulfil that responsibility as best I can. So the holiday in Bali is more than I need myself, but it's great for the wife and kids, and it's a wonderful opportunity to enjoy God's creation. And so is the pool. It can be a real focus for inviting friends over and socializing. It adds value to the house, too, which in the end is not for me but for the kids. I need to maximize its potential because it's an asset that I'll be passing on. So when we did the kitchen renovation last year, I decided we shouldn't skimp but get the best European appliances, because after all it adds enormously to resale value, and that's just a good use of money."

And so on, and so forth—until I find myself leading a life of affluence quite identical with my non-Christian neighbours, and quite devoid of any evidence that being a disciple of Christ has made the slightest difference. We find ourselves, like the Preacher of Ecclesiastes, meaninglessly accumulating wealth and possessions which are transitory and uncertain, and which ultimately yield no satisfaction.

All the same, it's a line of reasoning that is seductively plausible, and half true. We *are* responsible for the welfare and sustenance of our families, and we *should* be prudent in our use of resources. Where it fails is that it makes the comfort and financial prosperity of our families the determinative factor in most of our financial decisions. Instead, the determinative factor should be the ultimate goal—to follow Jesus Christ through suffering and death to glory; to obey him, to serve him, and to love others enough to want the same for them.

If we are seeking his kingdom, and following his footsteps, this will be reflected in how we use the money God has given us. What does the way you are using your money say about your priorities as a disciple first above all? What example does it set for your children about discipleship? Remember, your children will watch what you do, and learn from it, for good or ill. What are you teaching them by the way you use your money?

The same practical exercise we undertook with time (above) can be done with our finances as well. Which are the fixed expenses and which are variable? Are the fixed expenses really as fixed as we make out? And how does the way we allocate the variable amounts reflect our priorities?

5. Remember the 10:10 principle

Ecclesiastes 10:10 says:

> If the iron is blunt, and one does not sharpen the edge,
> he must use more strength,
> but wisdom helps one to succeed.

I think this might have been where management guru Steven Covey got one of his Seven Habits from. Wise people take time to 'sharpen the saw'. They recognize that it's important to keep themselves sharp and effective, so that they can do the job efficiently. In management terms, this usually means investing in professional development, going on courses, eating and exercising well, and so on.

As human beings, fathers would do well to heed the 10:10 principle. We need to keep ourselves fit—mentally, emotionally and physically—if we want to keep juggling all those balls over the next 10, 20, 30 years. However, *as disciples*, it's also vital that we keep sharpening the saw. No matter how long we've been on the road, we still need regular sustenance.

The three main sources of this sustenance that God has provided for us are:

- feeding from his Word;
- expressing our trust of him in prayer; and
- being encouraged and sharpened by others in fellowship.

These three are the staple diet of disciples, and we mustn't neglect any one of them. If we do, we'll end up 'blunt' and very tired. Our pace will slow, and eventually we'll fall to our knees in spiritual exhaustion.

There are numerous practical ways to keep refreshing ourselves from these three sources. At the moment, my 'saw sharpening' looks like this. I aim to:

- read and pray from *The Daily Reading Bible* at least three times a week (see inside back cover for details about this handy resource);

- pray most weekday mornings during my 15-minute walk to work, and with my wife for a few minutes before bed at night; and
- attend church each week, plus meet with a small group of men once a fortnight for prayer and study.

To me, that doesn't sound very ambitious, but I still find myself failing to keep up one aspect or another. However, it's a plan, and it's achievable (at least most of the time).

It doesn't matter very much what programme you come up with. It doesn't have to involve 45-minute quiet times every morning, or weekly accountability sessions with your spiritual mentor. The important thing is that you plan something, and follow through on it.

• • •

THE QUESTION WE have been asking is: Does God have a purpose for fathers? What's it all for?

So far, we've seen the first part of the answer, namely that our purpose in life is not determined by ourselves, as if we were self-created. To reach our destiny we must say 'No' to that foolish lie, and follow Christ as his devoted disciple, walking in his footsteps down the road to the heavenly Jerusalem, and facing with courage all the suffering and hardship that will come along the way. As Christians we have said goodbye to our past lives, and we are now focused on one goal, and one destination. As Paul puts it in Colossians 3:

> Set your minds on things that are above, not on things that are on earth. For you have died, and your life is hidden with Christ in God. When Christ who is your life appears, then you also will appear with him in glory. (Col 3:2-4)

But there is a second part to the answer as well. It's not really a different or a separate answer, but it deserves a chapter all to itself.

ENDNOTES
5. John Calvin, *Institutes of the Christian Religion,* III.7.1.
6. From Malachi 1:2-3, quoted in Romans 9:13.

CHAPTER 10

TAKING THEM WITH YOU

BEING DISCIPLES OF Jesus means striving to live as he lived, and especially to love as he loved. The Bible makes this point often.

In Ephesians, for example, Paul repeatedly talks about the Christian life as a daily 'walk' or journey, in which our lifestyle should reflect the fact that we've thrown our lot in with Jesus:

> For we are his workmanship, created in Christ Jesus for good works, which God prepared beforehand, that we should **walk** in them. (Eph 2:10)

> I therefore, a prisoner for the Lord, urge you to **walk** in a manner worthy of the calling to which you have been called, with all humility and gentleness, with patience, bearing with one another in love. (Eph 4:1–2)

> Now this I say and testify in the Lord, that you must no longer **walk** as the Gentiles do, in the futility of their minds. (Eph 4:17)

> Therefore be imitators of God, as beloved children. And **walk** in love, as Christ loved us and gave himself up for

us, a fragrant offering and sacrifice to God. (Eph 5:1–2)

… for at one time you were darkness, but now you are light in the Lord. **Walk** as children of light (for the fruit of light is found in all that is good and right and true), and try to discern what is pleasing to the Lord. (Eph 5:8–10)

Look carefully then how you **walk**, not as unwise but as wise, making the best use of the time, because the days are evil. (Eph 5:15–16)

There are certain ways we *shouldn't* walk—in foolishness and darkness, as the rest of the world does in the futility of their minds. And there are certain ways we *should* definitely walk, which can basically be summed up as "all that is good and right and true" (Eph 5:9).

A key component of this Christ-like walking style is *love*. All our interactions and relationships with others should be driven by love—whether it's in putting up with each other's bad habits and weaknesses, forgiving one another, being kind to one another, speaking to one another truthfully, or sacrificing our own interests for the sake of others.

This was, after all, the essence of Christ's long walk to Jerusalem. He wasn't going there for a holiday. He was going there to die for you and me, in our place, as an atoning sacrifice for our sins—to love us and give himself up for us, as Paul says.

That's what love is: *it is intentionally seeking the good of others, regardless of whether they deserve it, and regardless of what it costs.*

Rather like 'hate', we tend to think of 'love' as an emotion or feeling towards someone else. Primarily, however, 'love' as the Bible talks about it is an attitude or commitment towards other people that seeks their good and their welfare.

What this means is that as we walk the road of discipleship, we won't do so with blinkers on. We won't walk head down, focused only on reaching the goal ourselves. If we're to walk as Christ walked, we will constantly be seeking to love others, to promote their welfare, to help them, to sacrifice our own comfort and interests for their sake.

In practice, this means that we'll always be seeking the good of others, rather than ourselves—in our work, in our daily business, at church, in our family relationships, and so on. In fact, 'seeking the good of others' (i.e. 'love') is a very useful way of thinking about our daily work. As we plod up the stairs and into the office for the 3746th time, and face another nine or ten hours doing stuff that is 80% routine, how do we face it? Why are we doing this? Ultimately, the answer must lie in our desire to serve others, not in seeking our own interests. The primary motivation for work, as the Scriptures describe it, is love. Love will drive us to work in order to nourish and sustain ourselves and our families, and thus not be a burden on others (see 1 Thess 4:9-12; 2 Thess 3:6-13). Love will also drive us to work in order to serve the community—e.g. by providing them with ways to look after their money safely, by driving them around in our bus, by healing their bodies, or by selling them food. We labour primarily for the sake of others. To regard our work as being really about *ourselves*—our career, our satisfaction and fulfilment, our importance and recognition, our wealth—is to make the mistake that many people in our world routinely make. To pursue happiness, wealth and satisfaction through work, as The Preacher Man reminded us in chapter 7, is a doomed and fruitless exercise. Satisfaction in our work is a great blessing, if we are fortunate enough to have it. But it is misguided and elusive as a goal, and rarely achieved (see Eccl 2:18-26).

Love means seeking the good of others, and it should be the motivation, the driving force and the goal of most things we do in life. Of course, the best and most enduring good we can seek for others is that they too would turn to Christ, and walk with us on the road; that they too would abandon the fiction of controlling their own lives, as if they were God, and would find their purpose and meaning in life in Christ, and in being his disciple; that they too would continue faithful to the end, and receive the crown of glory in the kingdom of Christ. If in Christ we have found the purpose of our existence, love drives us to share the news with others, and to encourage and help them along the way.

To put it another way, as fathers our purpose in life is not only to be a disciple, but to *make* disciples. We want everyone, including our own families, to come with us down the road of discipleship, in following the footsteps of Jesus through suffering to glory.

This all sounds well and fine. Of course Christians want other people to be Christian too, and of course Christian fathers want their children to grow up as Christians. But we need to feel the weight of what we are saying.

Let's look at two implications in particular:

- what we want for our kids; and
- how we can take our kids with us as disciples.

What we want for our kids

Do we really want our kids to be disciples of Jesus? Do we really want them to come with us on the road? What Christian father would not answer, 'Yes!'?

But we need to remember what sort of road trip we're asking them to sign up for:

- Are we looking forward to them being persecuted and ridiculed by school mates for standing up for what they believe?

- When they suffer hardship, trials, prejudice, rejection and mistreatment of various kinds, are we going to rejoice that they are earning their stripes as disciples of the Master who was treated in exactly the same way? Will we be thankful to God the Father for disciplining them as his children by sending them hard times?

- Are we going to congratulate them when they drop out of medical school to take a job teaching Scripture at the local high school?

- Will we be pleased when they decide to go to the mission field, and into the path of danger, insecurity and financial disadvantage? In fact, will we pray for them to do so?

How disappointed would you be if your son or daughter didn't end up in the kind of career you've imagined for them? You yourself might be a clerk in the public service, and you've always hoped that your daughter would get to university and find her way into a more satisfying and lucrative career than your own. Or you might work in a factory, and have always hoped that your son would get an apprenticeship into a good trade, like plumbing or carpentry. Or you might be a doctor who has always hoped that your son would follow in your footsteps.

But what if they turned out to be fairly average in ability, and didn't ever rise to any significant heights. What if they had a fairly dead-end job on modest wages? Would you feel you had failed?

Speaking personally, I would have to confess that my instinctive answer is 'yes'. If any of my kids, for example, didn't complete high school, and didn't go on from there to some form of tertiary education, I would find it hard not to feel let down. I would feel that not only had they failed, but that I had failed. If I'm honest, it's because I have several unspoken but very deeply held goals for my kids—goals that involve them achieving a certain level of education, leading to professional achievement, financial security, prosperity and (I expect) happiness. It's what I expect for them, and what I want for them.

But if I go back and re-read what I have written in chapters 7, 8 and 9, and listen to my own advice, I would see that these are false, foolish and ultimately unachievable goals. To be a disciple of the Lord Jesus Christ, the ruler of this world, and the one who holds the future of this world in his hands, and to love others such that they too become disciples—those are the first and most urgent priorities for every human on this planet, including my children. It matters *very little* whether they are plumbers, policemen or paediatricians, or whether they live in a mansion or a mud-hut.

Yet I find that the hopes and dreams I naturally have for my kids—absorbed as they are from the normal hopes and dreams of those around me—have lots to do with their educational, professional and financial success, and very little to do with their maturity as disciples of Christ, and their passion for his kingdom. I worry about what school they should go to far more than I worry about whether I am schooling them adequately as disciples of Christ.

This brings us to the guilt-inducing subject of teaching, training and discipling our children in Christ.

How to take them with us

Perhaps we should just admit, before we go any further, that we all do a less-than-perfect job in this area. Some of us try hard, but feel we are failures. Others hardly try at all, and would rather avoid the subject. But if we're going to be disciples, then we must be disciple-makers—because following Christ's example of love must mean desiring that others find their purpose and meaning (not to mention salvation) in him.

Let's step back and ask the more general question: How do you help someone else to become a disciple of Jesus, and to remain on that path—whether that person is your own child or your wife or your next-door neighbour? Humanly speaking, making or encouraging a disciple happens through:

- teaching in life;

- personal relationship and example; and
- prayer.

Teaching in life

It may seem like stating the obvious, but it is impossible to make someone a disciple of Jesus without teaching them what that means. Some fathers don't seem to grasp this basic point. They think that if they simply set a good example—which is important, as we will see shortly—then that's about all they can do. It's bound to rub off onto them somehow. This fails at two important points:

- For a start, it misunderstands the nature of Christianity completely. Christianity is not simply a lifestyle to be copied, just as it is not only a set of truths to be learned. It is relying on Someone as our Saviour and Lord, listening to him and trusting his words, and then obeying him day by day. It is both truth and action, knowing and living, believing and obeying. How can they believe, says the apostle Paul, if they have not heard (Rom 10:14)?

- It also sets the wrong example. A father who never speaks (or hardly ever speaks) about Christian things teaches his children a clear lesson: "Christianity is not all that important as a topic of conversation in everyday life". As day after day goes past, and you never open your mouth to talk to them about the things of God—whether informally, or in a structured way, what are you saying to them? You are teaching them a lesson they won't forget about the importance of Christianity in everyday life—or it's lack of importance, as the case may be.

If we're going to 'make disciples', then part of the program has to be "teaching them to observe all that I have commanded you", as Jesus said to the Twelve as he was about to leave them (Matt 28:20). This seems obvious enough, and we would rarely question it in relation to our friends or neighbours. If someone we knew had just become a Christian, and they said to us, "Listen, do I need to study the Bible or something, or get some input about how to live as a Christian?", can you imagine saying to them, "No, I don't think it's all that necessary; just hang around Christians a bit and do what they do. It'll rub off"?

For fathers, it's even more imperative. Our *responsibility* is to nourish and raise our children, and we have been given *authority* to teach and discipline them, for their good (remember chapters 3-5). Fathers should teach their kids about every aspect of life: from politics to shoe laces to how to catch a ball. Like Solomon with his son, fathers should impart wisdom and skill for living to their children. It's what fathers do—they teach their sons and daughters. Teaching our children the gospel is no different.

The Bible makes this quite explicit when it tells fathers to bring their children up "in the discipline and instruction *of the Lord*" (Eph 6:4). We saw in chapter 5 how this 'discipline and instruction' is a package deal, involving not just the imparting of content, but training in that content, including the use of rewards and punishments. However, we didn't say much at that point about the "of the Lord" part of the verse. How should we teach our children the things of God?

One of the best ways to answer that question is to listen to how God told the Israelites to teach their children in the Old Testament. The classic passage is in Deuteronomy 6. Israel is perched on the edge of the Jordan, with the Land of Milk and Honey just across the river. As they prepare themselves to take possession of it—after 40 years of false starts—Moses gives them a good talking to. He reminds them of all that they've been through and the many mistakes they've made. And he urges and exhorts and commands them not to repeat those mistakes once they enter the good land that God is giving them. Part of Moses' strategy for promoting faithfulness and obedience to God is to make sure that the Israelites pass on their law and history to their children. He puts it like this:

> "Hear, O Israel: The LORD our God, the LORD is one. You shall love the LORD your God with all your heart

and with all your soul and with all your might. And these words that I command you today shall be on your heart. You shall teach them diligently to your children, and shall talk of them when you sit in your house, and when you walk by the way, and when you lie down, and when you rise. You shall bind them as a sign on your hand, and they shall be as frontlets between your eyes. You shall write them on the doorposts of your house and on your gates." (Deut 6:4-9)

Israel was about to enter a land with a multitude of 'gods' and idols, in which their devotion to the one true Lord would be tested. Listen, says Moses, there is only one God that you must love with all your heart and soul and might. Don't forget him, and don't forget these words of his that I am telling you this day. Keep them close to you, in your very heart. Treasure them, remember them, do them. Make them the centrepiece of your life, your family, your home. Write them on the back of your hand with a biro. Put post-it notes on the side of your computer monitor. Stick a whiteboard on the wall of your lounge room, and write on it: 'The Lord is God'. Just don't forget them, or depart from them. And teach them to your children.

This passage has a delightful emphasis. First of all, it urges the Israelites to have these things on their own hearts, and to be completely devoted to them—in other words, to be passionate disciples themselves. As we've already noted, fathers are disciples first of all. There is no way we can teach our children to be disciples if we are not committed to discipleship ourselves. Or to put it in Moses' terms, if we do not strive to love God with all our heart and soul and might, there is no way we will ever persuade our children that what we are saying to them about God and about Christ is important. You cannot hide this from them. They will see, and they will know. The first step in making disciples of our children is to keep walking the road ourselves.

The second step is to "teach them diligently". This, for many fathers, is the hardest step of all. We know we should, but everything seems to conspire against us finding the time and energy and motivation to do it. This is another area in which a little planning can save a lot of frustration. Sit down with your wife and work out how you're going to do it. Make sure you come up with a plan that *works for the ages of your children and your own current circumstances*.

For example, when the ages of our children ranged from 4 to 12, it was just not realistic to sit together around the table, with all five of them, and read a Bible passage together and discuss it. (I should add, the younger two are boys. Enough said?) At that stage of our family life, we needed to do things more individually. One of us would read to the boys, and the other to the girls, and then we'd swap over the next night. As I'm writing this, the age range is 9-16, and we can have some very enjoyable and fruitful discussions about Bible passages. We also have some noisy, fractious and utterly frustrating discussions, which involve certain persons being forcefully ejected, after which I turn my attention back to the rest of the group still assembled, and say with face still looking like thunder, "Now, what else does this passage say about patience?"

Because of the number of kids in our family, reading individually with each child every night has not always been possible for us. So at different times we've tried to have a short family time after dinner, with some prayer and perhaps a song or a memory verse, and then worked at reading the Bible individually with different kids on different nights of the week.

Nor have we always been in a position to have some 'family Bible time' every night or every morning of the week—in fact, we've hardly ever succeeded in keeping that level of teaching going for very long. But it's much better to plan the three nights in the week, or the three mornings in the week, when you're going to do something—and then do it—than to feel paralysed and guilty that you can't have family devotions every day and twice on Sundays.

The format and timing and arrangement of how you do it can (and should) vary enormously, depending on your circumstances. There are also a wealth of options and possibilities for *how* you might deliver the instruction.

Here is a list of ideas that I've collected over the years from talking to different families about how they teach their children:

- For young children, try making a simple 'prayer book' that you can use as the basis of the family prayer time. Have six or seven big pages, with each one focused on a particular area for prayer. The one we have used has days for: our own family (i.e. prayer points for each other), our big (i.e. extended) family, thanksgiving for God's good gifts, people we know who tell others about Jesus (missionaries etc.), our church, the world. We've written a simple prayer for each page that we can say together, and Ali helped the kids add drawings and stick on photos of people we want to pray for.

- A variation on that theme is to make a deck of 'prayer time cards'—you can use those perforated A4 sheets of business cards that you can print on your inkjet printer for this. Put lots of different things to pray or give thanks for on the cards, plus some memory verses, some important questions worth discussing, or some written prayers—and then everybody takes a card and does what it says. Another form of this idea is simply to have a bag of photos, from which everyone pulls one out (without looking), and then prays for that person.

- Make use of the growing range of printed resources that can help you teach your children: from children's Bibles to family discussion guides to individual booklets that help your children read the Bible for themselves. (See the *Further Reading* for a selection of those currently available.) Don't be afraid to experiment with something, and to abandon it if it's not working. And don't always underestimate your kids, or assume that you know what they will like. I've recently been reading a children's version of *The Pilgrim's Progress* with my 9 and 10-year-old boys. I thought it might be beyond them, but they have loved it.

- The simplest method is simply to read a portion of the Bible, and discuss it together around the table. A little preparation for this goes a long way. One of the simplest methods is to read the passage yourself in the morning, for your own personal Bible reading, and then discuss it with the family that evening—having worked out just one or two simple questions or ideas to get the discussion going.

- The book of Proverbs has a special place in fathers teaching their children, because that's what Proverbs mostly is: it's the wise instruction of a son by his father. Try selecting just one meaty proverb, and chewing over what it means. We had great fun recently with: "Like a gold ring in a pig's snout is a beautiful woman without discretion" (Prov 11:22).

- Quizzes are also worth trying for variety. Pick up a Bible quiz book at your local Christian bookstore, and have some fun. If you choose your questions in advance, you can also choose one that makes an important point that you can dwell on.
- You might try reading a Christian book together every now and then—not as a staple diet, but as a change of pace. Kel Richards's *The Case of the Vanishing Corpse*, for example, is an enjoyable and informative way to talk together about the importance of the resurrection, and the strong evidence for its truth.

Regardless of how often you do it, and for how long, or what method or materials you use, the two vital elements are:

- that you keep on *diligently* talking to your kids about Christianity, and teaching them from the Bible, year in and year out; you'll have ups and downs, and purple patches and droughts, but just keep going. Don't give up.
- that you take the initiative in planning the instruction, and calling the family together when it's time. Don't leave it to your wife. I have a friend who insists that this is an infallible indicator of whether a father is exercising spiritual leadership in his family: if he is the one who initiates the family Bible and prayer time.

We've been talking about diligently instructing our children, but we need to notice something else from Deuteronomy 6 (which is where this long diversion into teaching methods started). Moses tells the Israelites not only to teach their children diligently, but to do so in *all of life*: "You shall teach [these words] diligently to your children, and shall talk of them when you sit in your house, and when you walk by the way, and when you lie down, and when you rise".

Teaching our children how to be disciples cannot be partitioned off into 15 minutes after dinner. It should be on our lips in every area of our lives. But here's the thing: if we are diligent about planning and carrying out structured times of teaching, the informal times will come. If our children know that Christianity is important, that we talk about it often as a family, and that it affects every area of our lives, then opportunities will arise to teach them informally and casually, as we drive them to soccer, as we tuck them into bed at night, as we help them with homework, and as we relax in front of the motor racing on TV. Sometimes we might initiate these informal opportunities, by responding to something they've said with what the Bible says about the topic—for example, I remember sitting on the edge of the bed one night, tucking one of my daughters in, and she said, "Dad, you know my friend Lucy? She got mad with me today because I said that the

Gay Mardi Gras was really wrong. I think that her mum is a lesbian". My daughter was 11 at the time. There was an opportunity not only to talk about the 'gay issue' together, but to talk about how to care for her friend Lucy; how to be sensitive and kind to her, and so on.

Children are insatiably curious. They ask questions. Many of the richest and (I think) most effective teaching times I've had with my kids have been in response to questions they have suddenly come out with. This is what Moses told the Israelites to expect, and he also told them to be ready with some answers. Later in chapter 6 of Deuteronomy he says:

> "When your son asks you in time to come, 'What is the meaning of the testimonies and the statutes and the rules that the LORD our God has commanded you?' then you shall say to your son, 'We were Pharaoh's slaves in Egypt. And the LORD brought us out of Egypt with a mighty hand. And the LORD showed signs and wonders, great and grievous, against Egypt and against Pharaoh and all his household, before our eyes. And he brought us out from there, that he might bring us in and give us the land that he swore to give to our fathers. And the LORD commanded us to do all these statutes, to fear the LORD our God, for our good always, that he might preserve us alive, as we are this day. And it will be righteousness for us, if we are careful to do all this commandment before the LORD our God, as he has commanded us.'" (Deut 6:20-25)

What's that pile of stones for, Dad? And why do we go up to the temple all the time? And what's with killing all the goats and lambs? And how come we have to obey all these eating rules? My friend Og the Moabite says that bacon and eggs is the best food on earth—why can't I try some?

The Israelite father was to be ready with a basic answer for his son about why they lived the way they did. And did you notice that what he is to tell his son is basically the 'gospel' of the Old Testament—that God powerfully and graciously saved Israel, and rescued them from their terrible plight, and brought them to the land of safety and blessing so that they could live his way, in righteousness, all their days.

We need to be ready with answers too—not just the basic gospel answer of why we live the way we do, what God has done for us in Christ, and why the purpose of our lives is to be his disciples, but also some answers to the tricky ones that children are likely to throw our way. If you don't happen to be ready with a good answer when a question comes your way, that's not a problem. Just say, "You know, that's a fantastic question. I think we should spend some time answering that at our family prayer time tomorrow night so that everyone can discuss it." And that gives you a day or so to gather your thoughts, and work out two or three simple things to say.

• • •

There is no doubt more we could say about teaching our children, but I hope the general gist is clear enough: we need to teach our children in all of life, through instruction, casual conversation, and in answering their questions, if we want them to know the truth about Christ and to follow him.

But of course teaching is not the only thing we should do.

Personal relationship and example

Good teaching hardly ever takes place in the absence of personal relationship—which is a roundabout, double-negative way of saying that our relationship with the person we are discipling is supremely important. Again, this is true for anyone we are attempting to disciple, whether our workmate or our eldest child. It's true for a couple of reasons.

Firstly, it allows the other person to see our teaching in action, reflected in our lives. After all, the message we are seeking to convey is that Jesus is the King of the World, who has died to take the punishment for our sins, and to free us to lead a new life of godliness and love. It's a message that is supposed to change someone's life. If that new way of life is *not* seen in our own lives, then the message is either false (it doesn't really change people's lives) or else we are hypocrites (who teach something we don't ourselves believe and practice).

A wise older Christian man said to me recently, "I was born into a Christian home, and fed the Bible with the bottle. But there was nothing as powerful for me in my formative years as the example of my father, who died when I was 20. The reality of all that I was taught was tested in my mind by what I saw in my Dad."

With our children, there is no escape from the reality of this, both for good and for ill. Example is a powerful teacher. They will see and copy our successes and our failures. They will point out (with unfailing accuracy) the inconsistencies and fudges that we attempt. They will see us at our warts-and-all worst. This should spur us to put our own lives in order, and to make sure that we are practising what we preach.

However, we need not fear our failures or our ungodliness. We don't need to model perfection to our children; we need to model *progress in discipleship*. We should never feel we have to pretend to be perfect as Christians in front of our children, or to cover up our sinfulness. We need to show them what it is like to be on the road, to be a disciple heading towards the destination, to fall over, pick ourselves up, dust ourselves off (or rather be dusted off by the overflowing mercy of our Master), and to resume the journey. In other words, to make progress.

Personal relationships are also important because they build the kind of trust that makes sharing and encouragement possible. With our kids, as with anyone, this comes down to the simple fact of spending time together. If we hardly ever see our kids, we can't be surprised when they don't open up to us, and ask us questions, and share their lives with us. The time you take to read books together, play cricket in the backyard, and go for milkshakes at the local café, is valuable in its own right. It's part of the joy of relationships. But it also has a wonderful by-product—it builds a level of intimacy and comfort and trust that makes discipling someone possible.

Prayer

Embarking on the road of discipleship in Christ is not a natural thing to do. The impulse to say 'No' to ourselves, to deny ourselves, and to commit ourselves totally to him—this is not something that springs spontaneously from the human heart. The human heart is selfish and deceitful beyond measure. Paul describes our default state as "dead in trespasses and sins" and "by nature children of wrath" (see Eph 2:1, 3).

Ultimately, there is only one way in which a spiritually dead person can have any hope or any future. As Paul says just a few verses later: "But God, being rich in mercy, because of the great love with which he loved us, even when we were dead in our trespasses, made us alive together with Christ—by grace you have been saved" (Eph 2:4-5).

For this reason, all our efforts in discipling someone are useless and fruitless without God's work in their lives. And this is why prayer is such an important aspect of our ministry to other people. God uses us as his agents to bring his word to people, but in the end, without his gracious work to change the heart of someone to want to obey that word, there will be no progress.

One of the most down-to-earth, nitty-gritty, practical, nuts-and-bolts things we can do for our children is to pray for them. Regularly. It's not complicated or difficult to do. It doesn't take much skill. And we know—intellectually at least—all the reasons why we should.

Our lack of prayer for our children—like our lack of prayer for so many other things—stems from a lack of belief in its effectiveness. If we really believed that God wanted to answer our prayers, to work in the lives of our children to make them like Jesus, and that he incorporated our prayers in his way of doing things, wouldn't we always be praying? Wouldn't we suffer more from 'disciple's knee' than 'tennis elbow'?

In thinking through how we're going to 'make disciples' of our children, let's always keep in mind that it is God who really 'makes disciples', and never give up praying that he would do so for our children.

What if they won't come?

This brings us to a subject of anxiety for all Christian parents, and grief and agony for some. What if we do all we can to take our kids with us on the road of discipleship, but they won't come? What if God doesn't seem to be working in their lives, at least as far as we can see? How do we deal with the heartbreak of our children walking away from the Lord?

It's a topic we could take a whole book to discuss, especially given the strong emotions that it brings to the surface. As a starting point, let me suggest four important things that the Bible tells us.

(i) Our children are just like everybody else

It's true that our children are wonderful and special—although obviously yours aren't nearly as wonderful and special as mine—but in an important sense they are just like everyone else on this planet. We would do well to ponder the words of the Apostle Paul in Titus 3, because they apply to our children every bit as much as they apply to us:

> For we ourselves were once foolish, disobedient, led astray, slaves to various passions and pleasures, passing our days in malice and envy, hated by others and hating one another. But when the goodness and loving kindness of God our Saviour appeared, he saved us, not because of works done by us in righteousness, but according to his own mercy, by the washing of regener-

ation and renewal of the Holy Spirit, whom he poured out on us richly through Jesus Christ our Saviour, so that being justified by his grace we might become heirs according to the hope of eternal life. (Titus 3:3-7)

By nature, we are all sinful rebels against God, without hope and without freedom. That's how we all were until God washed us and regenerated us—that is, before he took our lifeless spiritual carcasses and breathed life back into them, not through anything we had done, but purely because of his astounding mercy. Our children will never be disciples unless God in his sovereign grace makes them come alive. And that is ultimately his work, and his decision, not ours—which is why we must continue to beg for his mercy upon our children.

(ii) Our children are privileged

All the same, children born into Christian homes receive a rich blessing from God. They have the privilege of being fed "the Bible with the bottle". They grow up hearing the word of God, and being prayed for by their parents (and relatives). They grow up experiencing the love and fellowship of God's people in their local church. Simply by virtue of their relationship with you as a believing parent, your kids have a rightful place within the covenant community, at least until they are old enough to decide whether they wish to stay or to leave (this may be what Paul is getting at in 1 Corinthians 7:13-14).

Given these influences, and given that this is the way God normally works to bring someone to himself, it is no surprise that a great many children from Christian homes become Christian themselves. The well-known proverb comes to mind: "Train up a child in the way he should go; even when he is old he will not depart from it" (Prov 22:6).

(iii) But it's not foolproof

However, Proverbs 22:6, like all the proverbs, is a canny observation of what usually happens in life, not an iron-clad promise or guarantee. After all, Proverbs also talks about the foolish son, who brings grief and anguish to his parents by making the wrong choices.

We need to remember point (i)—our kids are no different from anyone else. They are just as capable of stubbornly and foolishly rejecting the word of God as any other person. I'm sure you've known people, as I have, who have sat in church for years, heard sermon after sermon, and had conversation after conversation, but have remained cold towards God and locked up in their own selfish rebellion against him. And then there are others who wander in off the street, hear the gospel for the first time, and immediately embrace God's offer of salvation with open arms.

Now, coming to church for years and hearing lots of gospel sermons is certainly a good thing to do—in fact, a person who does this is far more likely, in human terms, to become Christian than someone who never darkens the church door and never hears the gospel. But it is no *guarantee*, just as all our efforts at family Bible times and prayer are no guarantee that our children will keep walking with the Lord.

The reality of the situation is that a certain percentage of children from good Christian homes don't grow up to be Christians. I was comparing notes with another dad recently who, like me, has a large family with the oldest in the mid-teenage years. As we talked about other Christian fathers we knew with four or five kids, we were hard-pressed to think of even one of them who hadn't had at least one child 'walk away' from the Lord in their late teens or early twenties. Who's to say we're going to buck the trend? Many of these Christian dads are the finest, godliest men you'd ever meet. Some of them are prominent in Christian leadership. If they can't guarantee a 100% success rate, what hope do we have?

This can lead to a certain degree of paranoia. You're gathered around the dinner table having a family prayer time, and your 10-year-old is lounging in his seat listlessly, making it perfectly obvious that he is bored rigid, and that he can't wait to get back to his computer game. It comes to his turn to pray, and he says in a flat uninterested voice, "Pass".

"Oh no!" you think to yourself. "It's started already. He's beginning to drift away. It's the first sign of spiritual disinterest! I'd better make sure I read the Bible three extra times with him this week!" Of course, the truth of the situation is more likely to be that he is a 10-year-old boy, tired after a long day of school, who was really enjoying his computer game until you pulled him out of it and made him sit quietly at the table for 15 minutes.

Those of us with children yet to reach the 'rebellious years' need to relax just a little, trust God, and keep working away at our teaching, example and prayer.

(iv) The blame game

Come the day when, God forbid, one of my kids walks away from the Lord, I think I know what my reaction will be. I'll blame myself, bitterly, for all my failings as a father and as a teacher. I'll (secretly) blame my wife for not backing me up more. I'll blame my work for using me up, and not allowing me enough time and energy to be a better father. I'll blame the youth group for not providing an adequate Christian peer group. And I'll blame God for being deaf to my prayers, and to my wife's prayers, and for not saving this precious child who after all *deserves better than this*!

That's when I hope and pray God will bring Titus 3 back to my mind (quoted above). God owes me nothing.

He owes my children nothing. Nothing, that is, except the judgement that we all deserve. Like my wife and I, and like everyone reading this book, the natural state of my kids is perfectly described by Paul's words: "foolish, disobedient, led astray, slaves to various passions and pleasures, passing our days in malice and envy, hated by others and hating one another".

In the face of this, you can't demand mercy. You can't make a claim on grace. You can only grasp it when it comes, with tears of gratitude.

Fathers whose children have given up on Christian discipleship describe the experience as one of the most 'intense' of their lives. It places enormous stress on your relationship with the child in question, not to mention pressure on your marriage. At the best of times, husbands and wives can differ over where to draw the line with a teenager, but under this added pressure those differences can be magnified. (She says: "Look, you're being far too strict! Do you want to drive him further away?" He says: "Well, maybe it was because we were too lax that we're losing him in the first place!" Voices get louder, doors get slammed, eyes get rolled.)

In the midst of it all, we need to remember that God has a track record of going after lost sheep and bringing them back. Many a Christian parent can testify both to the heartache of watching their children 'take a holiday from the Lord' in their late teens and twenties, and to the joy of seeing them return. But there's nothing we ourselves can do to *make* them return, other than continuing to do the three things we've talked about in this chapter:

- to teach and encourage as you have opportunity;
- to maintain strong personal relationships in which your example is seen; and
- to pray.

I won't ever stop thanking God for the gift that my children are, and pleading with him to have mercy on them, as he has on me. I won't stop striving to walk as a disciple of Jesus, and urging and teaching and training my kids to come along with me. But where we'll end up together is ultimately in his hands, not mine.

CHAPTER 11
BE A MAN

At the start of this book, I said that my aim was to change your mind about two things: *what fatherhood is* and *what it is for*.

I've argued that as a father:

- You are a powerful life-giver to your family.
- You are a loving and faithful sustainer of that life.
- You are a leader and decision-maker, who exercises authority in order to fulfil your responsibilities.

And I've also argued that as a father you have two key related purposes in life:

- Firstly, your purpose is to repent ('submit to the new government') and follow Christ, saying 'No' to yourself and to the sin that so easily weighs you down, and continuing bravely down the road to the destination—which is the glory of his kingdom.
- Your other main goal is to take your family with you.

We've looked at all these points in some detail, and tried

to tease out what they mean in practice. If you're convinced about these things, and take them to heart, then they will change you as a father. You will have a clear sense of who you are, and what your role as a father is. And you will have a set of goals that will shape pretty much everything you do in life.

What should be very apparent if you've got this far is that being a father, and pursuing a father's goals, is no easy thing. It will take strength and courage, patience and wisdom, endurance and faithfulness. It will mean being true to who you are when others are trying to put you in a different box or persuade you that you are someone else; it will mean being single-minded about your goals when others are trying to divert you, distract you or stop you dead.

It will mean being a man.

Of the many memorable sermons by Phillip Jensen I have heard over the years, few stick in my mind as clearly as the one given to a crowd of 3,000 at a men's convention which began with the story of Sam Rayburn.

Sam Rayburn grew up poor, picking cotton in Fannin County, Texas. In the year 1900, at the age of 18, he left home for college in the city. As he arrived at the railway station with his father, all Sam had with him was a small bundle of clothes. His father, who was a man of few words, took $25 out of his pocket and pressed it into Sam's hand. It was the family's entire savings, and as he gave it to him,

Sam's father said just four words: "Sam, be a man".

Those words were to shape the rest of Sam's life. After law school, Sam went into the Texas legislature and eventually became the Speaker of the House in the US congress. He was one of the longest-serving and most respected figures in modern American public life.

"Sam, be a man." There was silence in the hall as Phillip told this story, and repeated those four words. I think most of us were thinking the same thing: Are we allowed to say that, these days? Is it all right to 'be a man'? Because that's what we desperately want to be. We want to be men. We want to be courageous, and fight for what is right and good. We want to accept the blows and wounds that come our way, and not flinch. We want to be honest and straightforward and true, and join great causes, and win great battles, and pursue great loves. And more than anything we want to be able to say to our sons with integrity, "Luke, be a man. Nick, be a man".

There was silence in the hall. It was not only because we were wondering whether it might still be possible to 'be a man'. It was also because, as we looked at our own lives, many of us saw mediocrity. The closest we came to fighting a great battle was sitting in our arm-chair and watching *Saving Private Ryan*. The closest we came to joining a great cause was working in a cubicle next to dozens of other people in cubicles designing software for improving customer service in the hairdressing industry. We thought about our own lives, our commitment to Christ, our commitment to our wives and families and churches, and we pronounced over it all that most damning of descriptions: 'soft'.

Fatherhood is not for the soft, or the mediocre. It's an adventure, and a cause, and a battle. It will take all the strength, courage, resourcefulness, hard work and honesty that you can throw at it—not just for a week or a month, but for years of your life. The enemies will be weakness, dishonesty, selfishness, faithlessness, laziness, compromise and plain cowardice.

The kind of fatherhood we've talked about in this book will only be possible if you're prepared to be a man. That's what it takes to be a faithful father, a strong sustainer, a loving leader. It's certainly what it takes to be a disciple of Christ, who is prepared to suffer and die for his Lord, and who wants to take his family with him on the road. "Be watchful, stand firm in the faith, act like men, be strong", said Paul to the Corinthians (1 Cor 16:13). That's what Christian discipleship and fatherhood require.

It won't be easy. But few truly excellent things are.

So be a man.

FURTHER READING

BELOW ARE SOME of the books that I found useful in the preparation of this book, as well as some suggestions in other areas.

On fatherhood, at a more theoretical level

Richard S. Hess and M. Daniel Carroll (eds), *Family in the Bible,* Baker, Grand Rapids, 2003—an interesting selection of essays, of which Tremper Longman's on the Wisdom literature was most helpful.

Ken M. Campbell (ed) *Marriage and Family in the Biblical World,* IVP, Downers Grove, 2003—another selection of essays. D. L. Block's contribution on 'Marriage and family in Ancient Israel' is especially good.

Marianne Meye Thompson, *The Promise of the Father,* Westminster John Knox, Louisville, 2000—when I was formulating my three-fold view of what fatherhood was (life-giver, sustainer, ruler), it was a pleasant and encouraging surprise to find this book that had come to much the same conclusion.

John W. Miller, *Calling God 'Father',* Paulist Press, Mahway, 1999—Miller writes powerfully about the importance and consequences of 'male-centred reproductive biology' in the Bible's conception of fatherhood.

On fatherhood, at a more practical level

Steve Farrar, *Point Man,* Multnomah, Sisters, 2003, rev. edition—the first of Steve Farrar's warm-hearted, stirring books on being a husband and father, and probably the best.

Kent Hughes, *Disciplines of a Godly Man,* Crossway, Wheaton, 2001, rev. edition—wise, challenging teaching about getting the different aspects of your life under control.

Kent and Barbara Hughes, *Disciplines of a Godly Family,* Crossway, Wheaton, 2004—originally published under the title 'Common sense parenting', which summarizes well the strengths of this down-to-earth book.

Best children's Bibles

For 3-7 year olds: *The Beginner's Bible* (Zondervan)
For 7-11 year olds: *The International Childrens' Bible* (Authentic Media)

Bible reading resources

Table Talk (The Good Book Company)—a series of discussion guides for family Bible times.

eXplore the Bible (XTB) (The Good Book Company)—daily Bible reading material for seven to ten-year-olds.

Discover (The Good Book Company)—daily Bible reading material for 11 to 14-year-olds.

The Daily Reading Bible (Matthias Media/Good Book Company)—a series of portable daily Bible reading books, each one containing 60 readings and the Bible text.

Who are we?

Ever since we opened our doors in 1991 as St Matthias Press, our aim has been to provide the Christian community with products of a uniformly high standard—both in their biblical faithfulness and in the quality of the writing and production.

Now known as The Good Book Company, we have grown together with our partner Matthias Media in Australia, to become an international provider of user-friendly resources, with Christians of all sorts using our Bible studies, books, Briefings, audio cassettes, videos, training courses and events. Call us for a free catalogue of all our resources. Or visit our full-featured website at **www.thegoodbook.co.uk** to browseand purchase our resources online.

| ☎ 0845 225 0880 | Elm House, 37 Elm Road, New Malden, Surrey KT3 3HB | FAX 0845 225 0990 |

Email: admin@thegoodbook.co.uk
Website: www.thegoodbook.co.uk